THE CHOCOLATE HOUSES WE BUILD

THE CHOCOLATE HOUSES WE BUILD

Okema Seven Gunn

7 Gunn Media

Arlington Heights, Illinois

THE CHOCOLATE HOUSES WE BUILD
Published by
7 Gunn Media
Arlington Heights, Illinois
email: 7gunnmedia@gmail.com

Publisher / Editorial Director: Okema Gunn
Cover Graphic Design by Okema Gunn
Book Packager: Qualitypress.info

Copyright 2023 © by 7 Gunn Media
Paperback ISBN: 979-8-9886767-0-6
Ebook ISBN: 979-8-9886767-1-3
Library of Congress Control Number: 2023912034

DEDICATION

To Mommy and Tristin
To my father Lawrence Owen Gunn
and for my friends Erica Faye Watson &
Amy Gooden who never gave up on me.

ACKNOWLEDGEMENTS

Special Thanks to the Gunn and Stevens family
And other family and friends who supported me along the way.
Yvonne Rose for editing my first book.
Thank you to Lisa E for getting me over the hump.
For Dave Coughlin and Ms. Fata who always
know where I've been.
To Yoli B who encouraged me to never give up on my dreams
To Joan and Carol for listening to my prayers and
accomplishments
To Brian Barnabus aka "Da Wildcat" for being a great friend
To Jaquaszian for helping me get through a tough year
To Uncle Alaric and Muteeat for your support
To Hosea Sanders for being a role model

CONTENTS

THE CHOCOLATE HOUSES WE BUILD

Dedication v

Acknowledgements vii

Chapter 1: Childhood 1

Watch the Girl, Twirl, and Swirl 2

Dig Deep 4

Some Hard Things 6

Oh Chi'ren, Oh Chile 8

Accepted 9

Runner Runner 11

The Weeping Willow and the Oak 12

Thumbsucker 14

Grilled Cheese and Tomato Soup for Yesterday,
Today, and Tomorrow 16

Touched 17

Teeth 19

Nightlight 20

Double Dutch 21

Chapter 2: Houses 23

The Chocolate Houses We Build 24

Tribute to the House of the King 26

Where I lived..27

The Chocolate Maid 29

London Chocolate Houses 30

Visions of Chocolate Houses 31

Dollhouse 32

Doghouse 34

Mansions 35

Movie Houses...36

Drive Ins..37

Lighthouse..38

Black Fire Houses 39

The Color Family 40

The Color of Dreaming 42

One-Way Street..43

Crooked Fence 44

The Trunk 45

Flooded Basement 46

Shelter-In-Place 48

Half Step Away from Homeless 50

Thugs, Rugs, and Carpets 52

When the Circus Comes to Town...................................53

Chapter 3: Culture and History 55

I'm Braided and Beaded...56

Sizzlin' Fry Hair, Sizzle Curly Girl Pop 57

Point of No Return..59

Empires Fall...61

The Audience and the Wolf 62

Afrofuturism 63

Black Aunties 64

Big Belly, Little Belly 66

Hunters and Gatherers 67

The Griot Voices 68

Gumbo 70

Black-Eyed Peas 72

Jazzin' Time and the Blues 73

Finna 75

One Monkey Don't Stop No Show 76

Tryna Make a Dollar Outta 15 Cents 77

You Do Too Much 78

A Hard Head Makes a Soft Behind 79

I'll Give You Somethin' to Cry About 80

I'll Knock the Taste Outta Your Mouth 81

3 Strikes and You're Out 82

I Wasn't Born Yesterday 83

After Dark 84

Ace Boon Coon 85

The Black Greeks 86

Clap Back 87

Baby Mama and Baby Daddy 88

At the BBQ, Not the Picnic 89

Barbershop 91

Cocoa Salons 93

You Ain't Worth 2 Dead Flies 94

Kwanzaa Time 95

Easter 96

Holiday Hissie Fit 97

Juneteenth Mind 98

Paper Bags 100
Tap Shoes 102
Black Vinyl 104

Chapter 4: Politics and Money 107

Guns, Games, and Lollipops 108
Blood and Taxes 109
Missing Black Girls 110
How the Cocoa Bean Relates to the Vanilla Bean 111
Teacher with a Handgun Spells M-U-R-D-E-R 113
Death of a Jogger 115
I Can't Breathe 117
Black Mama Sable 119
Black Cop 122
Breonna T. 123
Black Man's Burden 124
Black Flies Matter 126
Stimulus Check 2020 128
Word on the Street Is 130
Smuggled Chocolates 132
Protestors, Rioters, Looters 133
Put Your Ballot 135
Pandemics and Pandemonium 138
Cages and Boxes 139

Chapter 5: Reflection and Love 141

Wind Turning Pages 142
When You Go 144
Selfish Flower 145
The Best of Us 146

A Man of Debate 147

Heartbreak...148

The 7 Year Man..149

Animal 153

I am, We Are 154

Courageous 155

Vision...156

The Billboard...157

Looking for a Black Man Unicorn 158

Many A Night with A Man in Shining Armor.....160

Little Girl You Don't Live Here Anymore 161

Manchild Manifesting...162

Chocolate Chile Anthem......................................164

About the Author 166

Chapter 1
CHILDHOOD

Watch the Girl, Twirl, and Swirl

Watch the girl, Go twirl and swirl
In a tutu,
Salmon, sea green, lavender,
Cream or powder blue.
In a poodle skirt or flared dress
With unfurled silky ribbons in her hair.
Radiance of sun, warm summer glaze
Whispering wind.
Peppermint-striped, polka-dotted,
Cotton candy or crimson,
Lemon, or plum-colored hula hoops
'Round the waist, 'round the middle
Don't have time to answer any riddle.
Concentrate or mind-free twirl,
Chocolate, caramel, or vanilla girl.
Watch the Girl,
Go twirl and swirl.

Olympic sport with hammer
Throwing and circling strong steely metal momentum
Determination of smooth bronze discus ready for the taking
In a dance, she leaps and pirouettes gracefully.
On the floor, balance beam, uneven bars, or vault.
Assuredly worth her salt.
High and lofty, time for the sublime.

Charades
For practice in parades
She throws and twirls the baton,
Whips the flag, flips the flag, dead on.
Waits to catch, eyes to the sky, head lifted high.
Looming, Spinning Jenny or color guard girl

With golden brass buttoned jacket
White or gold marching boots.
Watch the girl, twirl, and swirl.

Nothin' to tweak
She's on fleek,
Perfect streak.
She slays the modeling runway
Yesterday and today.

In the park,
Turning on an old tire swing
Connected to chains above or threaded rope ring
'Round and 'Round she goes
Not in the throes,
Dizzy, frizzy, silly, or calm
Sun catches and cascades about her.
Sometimes alone, sometimes with an audience.
She's grinning, spinning,
Beginning to become
Intertwined with the twirl world.
Watch the Girl, Twirl, and Swirl.

Dig Deep

Dig Deep, Alas
The cold metal gate,
Mother told me never to
Cross that fate.
Little boys and little girls
Jump the fence
How quickly they come home
Before dinner.
We wait atop of the fence
Barbed and pointy.
Someone is coming
Silence. Pause.
As we crossed into the
Neighbor's backyard,
Creeping and crawling
Lurking, Slinking
Leaving footprints.
Foraging through gardens
Picking leaves and flowers,
Snapping twigs,
Stomping through the tulips,
Violating Property
Along the way.
Return home.

We hopped the fence
Dived, somersaulted
Over the cusped fence
With no remorse
Only I took the fall.
All played the game.
Barbed wire fence
I cut my thigh down deep
To white fat parts. It stung.

Kids all split. Time to go home.
Last one back is a rotten egg.

Mother was not pleased
When she saw my puncture wound.
Big brother told. Snitched.
Shrugged shoulders.
Busted.
Spoiled the fun.
I was heated, angry
For the big payback from
Another time.
No skimming lakes or ponds
For Me.
No swimming pools for weeks.
I still remember. I still own that scar.
I'm older and wiser now.
I remember how much it hurt and I cried.
Now I cry about other things, but I wish
I could go back and visit that ripe age of 10.
Going back, my childhood years
Don't seem so cold. Because I'm old. Older.
I'd tell that girl a thing or two tho'.
Set her straight
Give her the knowing.
Teach her a thing or two.
Protect her from the bite.
Shelter her from the winter's cold.

Now I tell my old self that...
Mindful young ones and oracles find
Mostly solace in summer.
It's the heat that makes them bold.

Some Hard Things

AMBER was just tan or brown
Like autumn and lumber, fossilized resin
Crunchy fallen leaves and crisp bacon
RED was just Washington apple crunch,
Round robust bell peppers,
Roaring red fire engines,
Searing hot blood, pumping through
My veins in anger.
It was stop sign and not go.
ORANGE was the celestial
Sphere that appeared upon the horizon
Like a ball of fire, blistering skin,
A hard harvest pumpkin to be thumped
When ripe or left out and
Laid on tray for sweet potato pie.
And the blaring warning construction sign for traffic.
YELLOW was my fear, set apart,
Embers of a blazing fire
Bright fluorescent marker
Infected puss.
It was caution and not go.
BLUE was the stiffness of my new fresh denim jeans
Vibrant ocean coral
Glowing sapphire that I was named after.
Thistles, Hummingbird songs, and whistles
Poisonous Amazon Dart Frogs
Pigmented azul-colored lobsters
The blue-eyed demon that broke my heart and the tears that followed.
PURPLEY things like: eggplant,
Artichoke leaves, amethyst stones
Raisins left out in the sun
Lavender and lilac tones.

GREEN was just jumping, frolicking
Grasshoppers,
Pistachios, hot and mild peppers,
Prairies and rolling meadows,
The way of sprouts and abundance
Crinkly or creased dried bills in my pocket,
Grandmother's emerald locket.
The signal for growth and Go! Go! Go!

Oh Chi'ren, Oh Chile

Oh Chile, Don't you know
At 6' o'clock the rooster crow
Get up early. Don't be late.
Off to school
Now find your gate.

Mind your manners
Learn in school
Sit up straight
Follo' Every Rule.

Oh Chi'ren,
Perfect Chile
Perfect Smile
"Spare the rod and spoil the child"
If they stray
Then they run wild.

Oh Chile
Don't you see
Straight home from school
Right after Three.

If old laws make the case.
They cover rules at every base.

Accepted

It doesn't matter how much
My heart aches and wails
Moans
She never accepts me.
It's not accepted.
My heart cold on a platter
Splattered
Ventricles pumping.
I can't scream
Or cry because
There's not much left.
No breath. No sound.
It's cold steel
That I feel
Metal in my mouth.
Blood.
I bite down hard
Grit my teeth.

I'm falling down
Descending fast,
Sinking into the night
Into the clay earth,
Into the sunset
Coming up through the
Soft foam of the tide
Of the beach, then at moonlight.

My heart is cold
Sometimes like weathered leather
Hard-boiled, thick-skinned
Because

Hers is cold, mother
Trying to be bold
Other mother trying
To break free
Is she waiting for me
On the other side of We?
In an alternate place
She calls me and I come
The weather is sunny
And bright. We embrace on the shore. Evermore.
Clear and unshrouded veil.
She meets me in that other place.
On the other side….
Other mother.

Runner Runner

I've never seen a runner runner
that loved to run so much
So fast, since he was a boy.
He'd run and run and
make sure he won.
But never for lack of fun.
A runner runner
called Gunner Gunner
couldn't make it any funner
Then to be jolly and enthusiastic
even in his eldest of ages.
He'd beat the odds of the disease
of big C twice.
So it was so nice
to see him recover and run thrice.
To travel to the states and
countries
Behold hills
Valleys, mountains, deserts and prairies.
Little towns, Big cities to travel.
In the extreme heat or on a gusty day.
Register to compete as an athlete.
50m,100m, 200m, 400m, 4 X 100m
To be number one
Champion.
"Fast gun", they said.
My father fast runner runner
called Gunner Gunner.

The Weeping Willow and the Oak

There was once a brother and sister
none alike,
The main tree in the yard was tall and lived for many years
Towered over the house.
Neighborhood children and I swung on its
weepy limbs and branches.
It was dying.
One year the black beetle bugs had gotten to it.
The Oak tree in the backyard
Hanging over the house kept us company
Kept watch during the night and would never leave us.
Gave us shade in spring and summer,
Gave beautiful red, orange, gold
in fall and stood by
when barren and
frost and snow came
and then the dew in spring.
Its sister the Weeping Willow
got cut down one dreary spring day.
Strange men came and cut and axed its trunk.
For many years it was a stump and we counted the years
and its many rings.
We sat on the stump and pondered like Plato.

The trunk and roots remained.
Finally, mother got tired of looking at that old stump.
Men came again and pulled at the roots and hacked.
They came with diggers and shovels, loud heavy machines.
Out came the roots of that old Weeping Willow,
Sister that we had been swinging from.
Mother replaced it with a mound of dirt
and Hydrangeas,

that bloomed only in the summer and
When I look at them,
I remember how beautiful sister was,
how sad she was when she had to go.
And all of the children in the neighborhood swarmed about her,
She had brought us all together at a point in our childhood...
Brother Oak still there. Still here.
He survived the cutting of other trees,
Watched over us.
Observing skunks and rabbits eating grapes on the vine,
Opossum possibly at the garbage,
Akin to chopping down a cherry tree,
Death of sickly Peachtree.
That old brother Oak tree survived them all
And was a nice home to many birds' nests.
I told mother never to cut him down.
Be faithful to him,
as he has been for us.
Strong and enduring.

Thumbsucker

For the longest time, the beginnings.
I can remember sucking my thumb
And biting my nails.
I guess Freud would have
called this Oral Stage
Piaget would have called
this Sensorimotor Stage.
Others might say different.
Eventually, thumbsucking
Subsided.
I believe food took over
as a remedy,
as the other habit.
as the other mother.
I'd rather be a thumbsucker
than an obsessor of food.
Behind closed doors
You can do anything
Like stuff your face
But you cannot hide
Or peel off fat
Or fatter.
It follows with the latter
Of rude conquests of
Folks that chatter
And vile rumors
Of things made up.
Judgmental
To make another
Sister or brother
Feel good or better
by verbal battering banter

Full of air, pneumatic
Thumbsucker, won't you come back?
It has to be something
To replace you too.
This addiction I'm having
This longing or craving I'm feeling
needs resolution.... Or is it deep, deep, deeper?
In my subconscious
Go and find her. Can you see her?
Thumbsucker won't you come back home?
Every once in a while, I bite my nails when nervous and
See thumbsucker, but I only wave hello.

Grilled Cheese and Tomato Soup for Yesterday, Today, and Tomorrow

My mama always
Likes to make
Grilled Cheese and Tomato Soup
When it's cold
Or on a rainy day
A tradition from my grandmother, too
Memories from her childhood
White bread or sourdough made crispy
From garlic, olive oil and butter
It's made with love
Comes from comfort and soothing places
To assuage all the woes and fears of the day
Three cheeses white and yellow
Feels magical
American, Parmesan, and Cheddar
Red soup smooth and creamy or chunky
With chopped tomatoes and spices
Like salt and pepper with diced onion.

Grilled Cheese sandwiches and tomato soup
Are for yesterday, today and looking forward to tomorrow
Soothing the now and the past
Promising illuminated future, Imagination
Curled up with a great book
Or decent conversation

Grilled Cheese sandwiches and Yesterday, Today, Tomorrow Soup
Is like a warm fuzzy, fleece or old chenille blanket.

Touched

It's that season again.
Late Fall
Early Spring
Winter.
Ah Choo.
Sniffles and belly aches
Boogers and goo.
Wash hands.
Don't touch rails.
Don't laugh at the Flu.
It very well
Could happen to you.
It will put you down
And beat you all around
Pound your head
Twist your guts
Wash the seats after sick
Because of sore butts.
Clean and scrub and sanitize.
Cover your mouth
Don't touch your eyes.
A word to the wise
One could get the Pink Eye.
I am touched
By many young children.
As a teacher
They don't know
For sure
How they get it.
They bring their lunch.
With the crunch and crunch
Germs from

Moldy sandwiches, fruits, and candy snacks
Often nestled in strange sparkly backpacks
This is not a tale.
I cannot lie.
I must survive.
Words I live and die by.
Touching papers, hands,
Pens, Pencils and glue.
Could definitely get the flu.

Teeth

Baby teeth
Are necessary
To be cleaned
The same things apply to apples and doctors.
Brush teeth often and floss.
Lots of sweets and treats
Might lead to decay.
When lost, the tooth fairy gives money under pillows.
I always wondered what she /he looked like.
I never caught a glimpse. Too fast.
In the pocket of my round yellow pillow.
Then adolescent stage.
Straight teeth require braces and metal wires.
Correction and time.
The cavity creeps into adulthood and then I had to deal with that.
First, it's lost teeth, braces, cavities,
then just old age and broken damaged teeth.

Nightlight

My nightingale won't you sing to me sweetly?
I can't live without you.
My nightlight.
You remain through my delta, my REM sleep.
Soft light to put me to bed
To sleep and navigate through my dreams
Sometimes keeps me up at night
I keep you close.
Like a warm blanket
Or milk and cookies to the children
Or hot cocoa
Or visions of
Terracotta colored
Gingerbread people dancing in my head

Or a nice hot cup
Of chamomile tea.
Before bedtime
Keeps the monsters and ghosts away
Out of my childhood closet.
You speak to me.
I whisper
A "Thank You,"
For keeping me safe. I know I can always
Count on you. Even When the bedtime stories
Have gone away long ago.
You're comforting, glowing, wonderful, youthful.
You've been a great friend.

Double Dutch

Double Dutch
Memories of chocolate girls
Twist and turn rope rhythm.
Skip, skip.
Jump in, Hippity hop. Jump out.
Piggy tails flyin', braids flippin'
Turn the ropes,
One girl at each end.
Hoppin' and Jumpin' with a friend.
Whap, Whop, Whip, Whop
Pause. Pulsating heat.
Whip, Whop
Then faster
1,2..3,4..1,2, 3,4
Rhythm
Jump and turn into the zone
Between the ropes
Running faster
Jump, Jump
Lift legs higher
Trickle sweat…
Blazing sun.
Laughter. Fun.
Spinning around chocolate swirl girl
For the culture
On the corner
Sweltering summer day.
Poppin' gum or fresh finished ice cream or popsicle.
Orange soda pop. Grape, or Strawberry soda.
Dark color tongue. Panting to catch breath.
Hey gurl. I got next.
My turn to jump…

Chapter 2

HOUSES

The Chocolate Houses We Build

We're created out of brown and red clay,
Creators of our day
We flourish in places where little chocolate children
Live in chocolate houses
With established Cocoa men and women
Taking care of their gingerbread
Sons and daughters, too.
Calm and quiet places
Serene scenes
No fear, no pain
Chocolate places, Cocoa-melanin spaces.
No yellin', nor cryin'
No redlinin', no overchargin'
Blockbustin' or gentrifyin'
Or lines drawn in the sand.
Approval about the stay
No rent, nor lengthy mortgage to pay.
Streets that comfort and raise
Fine upstanding chocolate people
Of various tints and shades
Who care for them
Praise them
Appreciate them
Value them. Value each other.
Lovely Land of opportunity
Bustling community.
Remembering Tulsa, Oklahoma
Rosewoods and Red Summers
We're back.
Black budding, building momentum, growing, sprouting up
The way it was once. Stranded in time. Preserved.
Thriving, Buzzing, Booming renaissance like Bronzeville and Harlem

Gingerbread, Cocoa, and Chocolate houses
Will stand the test of time as
We continue to remember and rebuild.

Tribute to the House of the King

He played trumpeter, a military man, a cop, a lover,
Number 42-Jackie Robinson, one of the first black major ball players
James Brown, Godfather of Soul
Thurgood Marshall, first black Chief Justice
And Black Panther King.

Chadwick was a champion among men.
A quiet, patient man of resilience.
I feel like I had known him before,
Like we all have felt his presence.
We learn from him royalty, humility, and fragility
Of life and precious moments.
Sometimes our time is short,
Like a shooting star across a bedazzled sky.

Life has a way of making space for the next
Generation to see and create their own light.
Here the King of Hearts and King of Spades are equal
In power. Balance.

The House of the King is remembered and revered.
It remains unblemished, unmatched, and incomparable.
His legacy is determination, absolute heroism, role model, and friend.
He is a lamp among the darkness that never diminishes.
He will be remembered as distinguished,
Just like my own beloved father, the Sagittarian, Mustang.

Where I lived

Where I lived
Is a magical place
Childhood springs up
Like a cool bubbling drink
From the brook.
I lived on Chestnut Street
Near Walnut Street
Close to Maple Street
Neighbor to Laurel Avenue
by Fowler Avenue.

It's peaceful and quiet
Surrounded, adorned and hugged
By Weeping Willows, Oak Trees,
Cherry Trees, and Peach Trees
and lovely gardens
that attract cardinals and ravens,
Opossum, squirrels, rabbits, and skunks.
Cars often buzz, whiz, and zoom by
Even on a dismal day.
The trees whistle with brother wind…
I wish I had a greenhouse.

Our sunroom records chapters of sunsets and sunrises
That glow of golden bronze and red
Filled with calm starry nights
Warmth in winter
Cool in Summer
Atmosphere
Perfect for writing in my notebook
Daybook, good-night book,
Cozy nook,

Dreams unbothered
Feet up, wiggle toes
Unashamed
Revelation and reward
I like where I live
Where I lived
Childhood home
Because I'm free…

The Chocolate Maid

Mother's sweat, likened to mother's milk lingered in
thick spring air.
Sweat mixed with sweet flowers
She planted one knee down.
Knelt in the dirt
Dug and planted flowers
Overall jeans in front of house.
The red door blaring back.
Gardening gloves and tiny multi-colored
windmill.
Planting Daffodils, birds chirping.
Ready to wash car in driveway when
finished.
Water hose ready.
She owned her space.
Chocolate woman in a special place.
Black hair pulled back, pink bandana.
Vanilla man drives up in a midnight blue car.
How much to pay for a
Chocolate maid service?
Who is the vanilla lady of the house?
Surely, not the hot chocolate lady of the house.
Mama is the chocolate lady that holds her composure,
Keeps the keys to the establishment.
She asks the vanilla man to get the heck off her property.
She becomes hot chocolate in her seething and steaming,
after vanilla man leaves.
Mama co-owns the chocolate house
Defends her space
While father is away at work.
She stands firm and proud to defend the castle
That the Chocolate people built.

London Chocolate Houses

In the beginning,
Chocolate houses were built
For the established upper class and elite
Sugar precious resource and cinnamon spice
As a treat.
Twice as nice as
Pure gold
Smooth and creamy
Chocolate hot for the good 'ole boys
With fancy threads and fabrics
Near London Bridge
Houses for meetings
With gossips and secrets
Bubbling hot chocolate
Buzzing and bartering,
Uppercrust, May be
A pretty penny or two
To engage
In such politics and economics
Creativity and occasional
Sword fight, a gentlemen's blight.
And drunken bets
The White Houses
Only for Vanilla Man
Not for the Ruby,
Chocolate, Cocoa
Carmel man or woman.

Visions of Chocolate Houses

It's turning into Fall
Bridge between Summer and Fall coming
Back to school
Pledging to change
For a new season
Transforming...
Leaves flicker from red to gold to bronze
Flames
Sway hither to and fro
Trees make shade among the chocolate houses
Downing the streets, boulevards, and avenues
A change is comin'.
Our chocolate houses brace for a sturdy whirlwind.
We deliberate and discuss details about
An election that is brewing.

Dollhouse

When I was a young girl, grandfather, the carpenter,
Built me a dollhouse
Of wood
Oh! The lingering smell of cedarwood.
I don't remember too many times playing with it because
It was rough and needed to be
More furnished, smoothed, and sanded down.
Somewhat functional.

When I think of the dollhouse
It reminds me of all the things I wish I had done
All the things I wanted to hold on to. My dreams and ambition.
Hug the dollhouse. Live inside. Sleep there. Stay there.
Locked inside. Hide inside with the little people.
It's still in the basement, hidden in the crawlspace, collecting dust
Filled up with memories with me the black girl, white girls,
    white boys,
My brother, black boy. Sometimes black girls and boys.

Every once in a while,
I still hear the laughter coming from the basement.
I think it's the dollhouse collecting memories
Like my father collected gold coins, buffalo nickels, and rare
    baseball cards,
Like my mother collecting plants for her garden, fancy wide
    brimmed hats, and Black Santas.

Dollhouse, keeping memories for some other children. Someday.
Longing for another family. It wants to play.

I think about the 70's and 80's and how things were so simple then.
Simpler than now. I'm glad I grew up with the dollhouse.

Even though I moved away. Grew up from it.
Got my own place now. Made of brick and mortar.
A big dollhouse.
Can't forget my first dollhouse and how it was a safehouse
Even with all its rough edges and unfinished business.
To me it was just beautiful, like my childhood home.
Because I lived there.
Good and bad memories alike.
And my chocolate family lived there.

Doghouse

My father was a man of many ambitions
He would stay out late and come in at unusual hours
No one knew where he had been. Gettin' into some trouble, I guess.

He wasn't great with finances, but he was kind, lighthearted
and didn't speak often
Unless he had something important to say.

I wanted him to be different. Not like all the men I knew. Set
apart. A man I could look up to.
He was a tough act to follow. And it's difficult to ever find
someone like him.

They say a man has certain tendencies. He wasn't perfect,
although in my eyes he often walked on water as a Superman.

He may have had his indiscretions in his lifetime, but I was
hardly ever exposed to them.
Kept them away from my brother and me. I guess many of his
quibbles and problems were between my mother and him, if
any.

They would often argue about things like most couples do:
about money, raising children, and maybe words or actions that
could not be taken back.

The days they argued, the outcome would be yelling and or
slamming of doors.

Over time, he ended up with less time in the doghouse as my
parents aged. And time dwindled away. Eventually, he was no
longer a young pup or a young mustang. But just seen as an old
faithful.

Mansions

"In my father's house there are many mansions".
If you believe in the heavens
They'll be a place
Where the angels reside
A city of paved golden streets
A place for you and I
The Promised Land
When I get there
They'll be no more pains
No competition for love or wants

I'll see the ancestors and loved ones
That I've been longing to reunite and commune with
Sunlight and jubilee will be our guide
Whispers and melodious songs of glory
Will echo throughout the dwelling places

My Father will be waiting for me
To return

In my vision
The old Souls
They'll all welcome me with open arms
In warm, luminous, shining spaces within the City of Gold
Where my castle of clouds will be overlooking a great river
of incandescent, living waters.

Movie Houses

Places of another time
Ancient relics come back to haunt
Remembrance of Hollywood
And independent sanctuary.
Filmmaker
Refined celluloid, new digital age
Coming prepared for the New Age
Of youth and the old
Changing world
Engaged secluded from the big city
Endurance of time and space
Work hard to finish the cut
Editing form
Projection and lights
Come to the surface
Of subconscious
Scrupulous attention to detail
Bubbling revelation
Collaboration
The wheels
Of innovation
Turning, churning
Conclusion
Lesson Learned
Final Cuts and drafts
On the Floor or fused
16 Millimeter (16MM)
Lights, sound, sights,
ACTION!
Surrounding people
With the Vision
Across the Silver Screen fulfilled
Projected.

Drive Ins

The Drive In's a place
For lovers and families
Automobile, automatics and manuals
Movie lovers peer at the
Larger than life screen, licorice
Popcorn, soda pop
Big speakers attached to car
Hotdogs packed, sandwiches
Hamburgers at the stand
It's crickets chirping
In the night awaiting the feature
Or double feature.
Silly commercials with popular
Jingles and tunes.
Air thick with anticipation and fingers tingle.
Summer chock full of hope and youthful dreams
Tribe of teenagers engulfs the scene too.
Patches of grass and dirt to roll up on to.
Vibration of speakers.
Memories full of lovebirds and youth.
Fresh nostalgia.

Lighthouse

Angels among us
Summer heats
Bubbling
Dusty road to nowhere
Longshore
Journey to the sun
Circles of ambivalence
Little Chocolate girl Lola finds a way
She's twelve.
Free to daydream whenever she gets the chance
There in Dakar for the first time
Visiting tour with family and friends
The highest point on the coast
I find my ancestors are there
A vision of bliss
Kemetic cantations
My Dakar
I reach out to you
My beloved
The way you remember me
Group of visitors, separated
From me.
I turn into her legacy, like a child.
I'm Lola
The little girl. I wear purple
And pink and white
Hair brushed back in two buns
We've gone on a trip
My first trip to Africa
Mother Africa
Across the mighty Atlantic

Black Fire Houses

What I learned
Keep the fire burning for justice
Fire engines
Slide down the pole
And put out fires and
Wild fires.
Drills
Sirens blaring
Yellow and black
Call to arms for alarms
The Fireman's pole waiting
Hold the red lantern
Fraternity of men and women
Foam distinguisher
Fire extinguished
Fire hydrant
Bursting pressure
110 Bat
Water supply
Neighborhoods, towns, and districts
Garage
May have office space, library, or trophy wall for lives saved
Fire Authority
Fire trucks rush out of the station
Dispatchers, hazardous materials contained
Rescue
Used for the enslaved and servants for fire service
Under command
At emergency's beck and call
Rare and courageous
Fire Brigade
Duty calls

The Color Family

Red Fred got it in his head
and said that he was led
to wed off of street cred.
Now Yellow Fellow
was shallow and began
to bellow about his
shallow brother
Red Fred
Who stole from the Fed,
that he be a shallow marshmallow.
Then came sister, Green Jean,
who loved the green bean, which
made her a lean mean machine
and the keenest I've ever seen.
Her twin Blue Sue cried boo hoo
in lieu of too few a shoe. A who
who stepped in poo poo while standing
in queue. She had no clue about
What to do.
Another set of twins was called Suave Mauve
and Mulberry Mary, who wanted to marry both
Larry and Harry at the dairy. They asked a fairy
that they not tarry about being contrary to their father named
Blackberry Gary.
Next oldest was Tan Jan who had a grand plan. She was a
Biggest fan of the Can Can and a man who ran for office to ban
anyone against the clan of Tan Jan.
She called upon cousin Golden Coulden and beholden she got
More than she bargained for. He was honest
and just and full of disgust promising never to
work with Tan Jan out the back of a van.
His brother Lee Coffee could see that he wanted

to be free of she. So, he paid a fine fee and Tan Jan
made a decree to let the man be free of the quandary.
Joe Snow came along to sing a song by the crow and what he
doth owe about the seeds he did sow and that he will bestow
upon his two cousins Golden Coulden and Lee Coffee.
Now, all can go and know that Snow is slow to anger! Whoa!

Hey! Hey! On a gloomy day in May Uncle Gray Jay began to
pray with his Bae Fay about the getaway or the stay from the
judge called Burgundy Ray.
There was a delay and that's okay
because Gray Jay had to say he had tooth decay as he lay.
The judge Burgundy Ray said "Nay" Gray Jay had to pay.
It was the way.

But then Jack Black came along to save the day. Yay!
The last of their kind was hard to find, he had a right mind to
take revenge on Tan Jan and her man.
So, Jack Black had a yak with a sack
and vowed he'd come back to take claim upon his name.
He had such a flair for giving a scare that none ever
challenged him again. Jack Black took a big stack upon his back
And all that was his and a girl named Liz and rode away that
day with all the spoils of the Clan.

The Color of Dreaming

Sometimes I dream in black and white, but mostly
I dream in color
I keep a journal by my bedside
to record my dream
although it may seem
A bit odd or funny
The most I can dream of is money
or about biblical lands of
milk and honey,
present horrors,
or joy rides, or apocalypses, or gigantic tides.

Sometimes they are fleeting ideas
like shooting stars.
They are a wall of woes from my day
That needs to be knocked down.
Recurring dream has a knack of seeping in,
the click-clack of creeping in,
lurking back into my psyche.
IT won't go away, as if to stay
Won't obey. When I tell it to leave
or give reprieve I
If I believe it will
Likely harm me or be the end of me.

It's always some sort of chasing or
Me facing a fear, but never actually getting to touch it.
I hope in the end I slay the dragon,
and the color of dreaming will be something of a pleasant notion.
When I tell it to my children
As bedtime stories and lullabies.

One-Way Street

A One-Way Street is a direct route
In one direction
Going in the opposite direction,
May be going against the grain,
You may find yourself turned around upside down,
Backwards and not forwards,

Distracted from the destination or the goal; sidetracked.
Not where you want to be.
I found myself on a One-way street in traffic
Turned around or upside down, backwards instead of forwards,
As travelers on the road looked confused.

It happened because I was not clear about my destination at the time.
Navigation compass out of whack.
I gathered myself together after this grievous mistake,
Pulled myself up by my bootstraps,
Adjusted my clothing,
Picked my face up off the floor and made a U-turn.

I was thinking, how did I ever get turned around or upside down
Backwards not forwards, wrong direction.
Further from the finish line?
Now facing in the right direction, I was equipped
To stay the course, remembering
What was my initial fixation of a sensation,
Overcoming distraction,
While using contemplation of the manifestation,
Of the completion of my journey
Down the One -Way Street......

Crooked Fence

I had always dreamed of a white picket fence
To surround our house
Our garden, our estate.
Growing up we had a barbed
Wire gate, like a crooked fence
Enclosed was a beautiful backyard
Memories of childhood chatter
Matters of the heart
Old see saw, swing set
Sandbox, sandcastles drift away
Don't drop your candy in the sand…
You can't pick it back up.
I then look to the
Young peach tree that leaned
Cherry tree uprooted and dead
Grape vine diminished alongside
The rebuilt garage
Crooked fence weathered
The storm forty years
Protection, not perfect
Stability, unconditional
Purposeful, sturdy
Holding the best parts
Of Family in
Keeping other parts out.
Crooked Fence,
Functional, Dysfunctional,
I come back to visit.
Not perfect either, but just right for us.
I'm home for a time.

The Trunk

On a long journey
The gathering of friends and family,
Pretty pictures in a frame
An old trunk passed down through
Generations
Old Memories flame
All grown up. Tears and well-wishers
Beginning- off to college
A sailor on an adventure
Into unknown torrential waters
Oh! The possibilities
Young girl grown into young woman
Boys to men,
Cut the umbilical cord
Mama's baby gone from the nest
Away from suckling breasts.
A new man, a new woman
Out to prove
Themselves worthy in a new era.

Flooded Basement

Range of water
Rains and pours
No one else to ease the pain
At first
My family and I implore
Are alone....

Then neighbors join us to help
To lend a helping hand during
The flood, during the pandemic
But not before the backyard
Begins to swell
Enter the stairwell
Water cascades down forcefully
Until full

Memories come crashing down
Of Paranoia dreams
Escalated, executed
Watery grave eluded
Squishing of rubber boots
Village bombarded by calls from residents
Sewers blocked up
Cry for help
Hoping the buckets and pumps
Of determination
Will ease the torrential rain
And waters will subside

Then they do
Water levels come down
Anxiety comes down

Soothing sounds surround
With sunshine around the corner
Waiting for rejuvenation
There's no quick fix
Just patience for the healing
And sunlight

Shelter-In-Place

Shelter-in-place
Time is up… No more.
Businesses ready to open doors.
Some have folded in. Caved in.
Disease closed us down.
We must build back up.
The nights of broken glass have come
Upon us?
Some brought by our brothers and sisters
Like a history repeating itself from
great wars
Chocolate children safe from the police, inside
And from the streets
When we leave the caves.
And for once there is death
Eluded on the street.
It's reserved for the domain.
But a time of
Rest and reset.
Blown away. Season of change.
Comes outside.
Cold leaves and summer emerges.
With the sun and sin brings heat and burden and black
And brown children
Chocolate begins to melt from pressure of outside
Forces
But chocolate children store up their homes and rebuild
Stick together
During the storm. Lockdown.
We've always had a difficult time.
My grandmother reminded me of the times of the
Great Depression as a young girl. Depression glass tells a story.

These times we in are new, different, but same.
We're fed up, grandma,
Mama from your civil rights movement. Did that work?
I wish you could see us now.
No Jim Crow gonna hold us back, no racists nor oppositional
      credences, or alliances
Now, young fledglings gone wild
Band together
We stand up too
We ain't takin' no prisoners
Nobody is at the wheel
I pray Jesus takes it.
Take the chaos away. If he's even listening to us.
This is a new kinda war.
Same, but different.

Half Step Away from Homeless

I was studying at the library one day in the suburbs.
That's when I saw her.
Brown skinned like me… in her 30's maybe.
There was a favorite seat by the windows in the corner,
by the fireplace.
One could see the beautiful trees that blossomed and had a
    wide perspective
Of the whole north side of the library among the collection of
    magazines and encyclopedias.
In Spring there is always a slight chill.

The woman's clothes were full of debris from past meals.
A dark sour odor emanated from her person.
She had 3 different layers of clothes like my aunt that had
    Schizophrenia
From Alabama. I met her with my cousin and her
2-year-old daughter.
Back then, it was the middle of summer.
I was making up classes my sophomore year of college.

Her homelessness made me feel awkward.
A sense of strangeness that I had not seen before.
Clothes were matted and braided in places.
She was slightly heavyset with workman's shoes.
Mohagany and sturdy.

I asked the woman her name, but I can't remember.
For all I know her name could have been
Cheryl or Tasha, or Keisha, Samantha, or Kadijah.
I had seen her several times before.
We were the only 2 black women frequenting the establishment.
I had come back from asking my mother

What I could bring as a gift without offending.
It was a $10 gift certificate to Micky Dees
A small kit with soap, lotion, and lavender body spray.
Something I treasured myself. I thought she could have been me.
If I checked out. I could have been her. In the lost and found bin.

I wonder how long she had been there.
If I was depressed, I pondered how I would go on.
How close I was. One or a Half Step Away from Homeless.
I never remembered her name. I was only trying to help.
She became frustrated with my interfering in her business
and prying.
That's when I backed away.
I never saw her after that.
I think she moved to a different spot.

Thugs, Rugs, and Carpets

Do thugs, sit on rugs and
carpets with pugs?
Do thugs sit on roads and carpets
and give hugs?
Do thugs rub a magic
lamp with the genie,
to make their wish
and vision to see?
Do they lay on a mat
with a fat cat
and beg coins off an aristocrat?

Do they rob and steal
just for the feel
or crush their heel
on a banana peel?
At the market with merchants
and thieves, with day-old meat
with dancing fleas?

Some are children who need to see
their bellies full of soft bread, dates, and jellies

Nomads and wanderers come to feast
and slay the beast of
the growl of stomach with unleavened yeast.
With a trained eye,
one must see the difference between the good kind
thugs, thieves, and debauchery.
Some are born poor, some poor, rich and fair.
But life is fixable,
By those that live life, especially without care.

When the Circus Comes to Town

I hope there are lots of animals
With a vanilla and chocolate clown.
Hope there are acrobats are bronze and mahogany too.
Full of sparkles, glitter and sliced cider and cotton candy
With sticky goo.
Hot chocolate, candy bars oozing with creme.
Chocolate and vanilla children's favorite dreams.
Lions that roar and elephant stands.
A silly clown parade with clunky old bands.
Rings of fire with a motorcycle man,
A long silvery snake that pops from a cannon.
A tight rope, disappearing act, dwarves throwing knives
and darts with an announcer that breaks into parts.
When the circus comes to town
I hope it's full of chocolate things
Barking seals and dancing bears with rings.

Chapter 3

CULTURE AND HISTORY

I'm Braided and Beaded

I'm the only black girl at school like this.
I'm like Cleopatra. Nefertiti, Hatshepsut
My crown has braids and beads
Swinging side to side,
back and forth, to and fro.
I go out like this.
I'm cold. I'm different.
I'm singularity. I'm exotic. I'm wondrous.
I'm from Kings and Queens.
I'm regal and elegant.
I saunter. I prance. I dance.
I'm braided and beaded, not bonded.
Untainted. I'm in the moment. I'm timeless.
I'm fearless. I'm power. I'm free....

Sizzlin' Fry Hair, Sizzle Curly Girl Pop

My hair braided and plaited,
Parted and greased.
Hot comb on stove
Is glaring with heat
Sizzlin' greetings.
I sit in the ready chair for straightening.
Back of my neck, perplexed.
Lean over ready for hot teeth.

Mama puts her hand on my shoulder.
Be still. I freeze.
She takes a piece of hair and goes to root
And then pulls sizzle straight.
Sizzle fry hair. Not fair.
Heat burn coming right up. I jump.

All the hairs must be straight.
I bite my lip. Grit teeth. Grab chair.
Think of anywhere but here.
Clinch my fists. Think of a place with sugar bears,
ribbons and rainbows. A cool water beach...
To take the pain away of the process
From Sizzle fry hair.

About an hour or so goes by, I am numb,
I still suck my thumb
fixed in a state
I come out of it to hear Sizzle. Pop.
I flinch when too hot. It won't stop.
Fried ever so slightly. Fresh burn.
Fried and laid on the side.
When it's over I lick my wounds.
Rub the scabs or soreness.

It was worth the pain
now I'm nappy no more.
I'm bone straight like a white vanilla girl.
Happy and not nappy?
Like her. I think?
I blink. I wink. I think hard.

Madam CJ Walker would be proud
Of my straightened curls. Of what she
Worked so hard to maintain on her domain.
As the first black female millionaire woman.
She don't judge. She don't budge
On her stance.

I'm taught that nappy is sometimes
good, sometimes bad. Tremendous.
Stir fry. Sizzle fry hair.
Steam. Bake. Broil. No lie. No lye.
Kinky hair goodbye for now...
No more nappy time right now...
For now...
Until my hair gets wet
Until I decide to coil up again,
Curl up Again.

Point of No Return

A small doorway that leads to the ocean.
Steps and rocks below.
Gorée Island
Chocolate bodies
Imprisoned in dark case
Shackled without air,
Separated perforated, paraded virgins,
Holding cells, no conditions fit for kings and queens.
Baked house clay, Big house cascading stairs for housed traders.
Traitors heavy laden with spirits
I feel ghosts and whispers in the darkness
Those shackled touched shoulder to shoulder, branded
Listened to silver tongues trading lives.
Traded for guns and for gold.
Mother, father, children down, to the ground
Crowns thrown and bound.
Trapped.
Darkness now
Help them.
Help them.
But we cannot touch them.
Reach them.
Teach them.
Angry.
Sinister rises up in me.
Clench my fists.
I want to pound them into the dirt.
Them that did this. Those that dared this.
Hurt them.
Them that caused this.
I cannot touch them. Reach them.
But I see them grins and laughs.

I've vowed one day the spirit gonna be free
and Lawd these traders gonna pay,
for the blood they done spilled.
We still tribal, still washed in the spirit and blood
of the Niger River, Nile River, Congo River,
the ancestor stream, Mother Africa,
But then they go. They go way down deep.
I see flowing waves among chaos
Beautiful. Pure golden light on the horizon,
but they never been free,
until they jump into the ocean or die of foul-smelling wounds.
That's the fate that awaits them.
Don't they know where they goin'?
But I look into the distance and wait for them
And know some day spirits gonna rise up,
Roam free and be accounted for at the pearly gates.

Empires Fall

They build. We rise. They tear down. We fall.
They build walls to keep men out, to keep God out
To keep men in

These governments and empires rise and fall
and have no recollection, no reflection of the history,
or years spent trying to be vain glorious in days gone past.
Tyrants and unjust rulers
Creep in because the people have no real leaders.
No real borders.

The people have allowed corruption to rule the day.
Sometimes we watch, sometimes we fight back.
But the ugly monster always prepares for battle.
Save his or her layers of pride. Despot or Despair.
His or her lair.

Make your case, make haste, upon the throne
If you dare.
If it be occupied by tyrants or corrupt
Unruly absolute king or queens,
It will be difficult to oust them,
Once they sit on the throne
and establish court in the castle.

The Audience and the Wolf

Speaking in front of an audience
Can be frightful and takes skill and practice.
Stare at a spot, clear and move around the room
But don't get stuck like a deer in headlights.
Make the speech. Throw the pitch.
Hold firm with your conviction.
Don't sway.
Grit your teeth.
Speak with fervor,
Pomp and circumstance.
You will see a bit of difference,
How your fears will disappear and dissipate
They will part like the clouds after a storm.
They lean in…on their toes…
Waiting intently to hear your story,
anticipating your every breath, your next move.
Move quickly or slowly,
No matter as long
As you do it with dignity
and determination
For the wolves that smell fear will surely pounce.

Afrofuturism

Black science-fiction
And Future Worlds
Yields
African Diaspora
Water builds life or
Reminds us of death.

Separation and war tears down,
Divides through,
Recognition
Builds up.
Bursting with energy.
Exploding into outerspace
A black future is circular and unyielding.

Where black skin,
Dominates, dictates, directs and survives.
Distinguished, Rhythmic, Psychedelic
Black and Brown fellowship continuum
Its very existence of soul and blackness
Of chocolate skin grows and thrives
Powerfully advancing into
A self-sufficient evolved
Community and technological society

Black Aunties

Black aunties brush and braid black kinky, curly hair,
Tell stories of Black Santa, Kwanzaa, and Black Sea Captains.
Magical lands very chill with books,
Go on trips and walked to the zoo,
Laughter, strange and fancy looks,
Amusement Park and rides,
Swimming pools,
Beaches and tides,
Summer BBQ in backyard,
Backyard fire and
Storming the play castle
Feisty rabbits and exotic fishes
Pet dogs that bark named Laila, Sterling, Ty Ty
Let them chase and hassle cats like Maxwell,
Play with Legos parts, and trains,
Help build fantasy rocket ships, and planes.
Pay for still drums and viola lessons,
See piano lessons and recitals,
Go to the library,
Gives hugs and pats on the head,
Ice cream chocolate bars and cookies
with birthday card cakes
Watch
Boats, helicopters, trucks, and automobiles whiz by.
Hear about trips with Popi on buses.
Winning snowshoe and running races and
Time with TeeTee's and dad at Mima's and Grandpi's house.
Macaroni and cheese, pizza and fried chicken, hot dogs,
French fries, family holidays,
Thanksgivings and Christmases and birthdays
Movies, watch cartoons while jumping on Mima's bed with the remote
Tears and laughter, boo-boos, and hurts

Bubbles
Security blankets
And baby seahorses with lullaby songs.
My how you've grown past the pictures and baby shoes,
Past inseparable cozy blankets.
I look forward to seeing you grow into adulthood.
To be a trickster, a jokester and expert of the field of your choice
and many more graduations, awards, and memories.
Your own voice.
You're all grown up.

Big Belly, Little Belly

A mother looks at her daughter and smiles
Another child is on the way.
Mother holds her belly.
Will it be a boy or girl?
To bring into this world.
Daughter rubs the round magic belly
and makes a wish, poked out knob.
Little hears something jump. In Mama's belly.
Looking at her own little belly.
She wonders someday about the becoming of a Big Belly.
It is a wonderful thing.
It don't come from the stork,
Or basket, or at the front doorstep
Or magically appears. It comes from Big Belly.
Mother and father meeting
She must be excited about the birth of a new child.
Big sis', Little Belly must be ready,
to share her things with the new arrival.

Hunters and Gatherers

There are those that seek to
Hunt their prey farm and fish,
Deer, duck, goose and gander.
They love to game and feast upon the bow and the gun.
The toil
Makes the blood boil
Inside the running of the meat
With a joyous defeat of prey.
Fisherman will conspire to catch
the fish with the wish
To be the finest catch and release hand in the land.
Farmers know what they know
About plants
What will spoil and what will grow
when the winds blow
from the soil of abundant lands.
They washed their hands of killing game,
For the role has no shame,
upon planting, filing, shucking, and plucking,
the greens and the vessels.
But when they sit down to eat
They all eat the same.

The Griot Voices

In the village, he or she is studied with oral traditions,
of stories and fables of magnificent creatures,
kings and queens, peasants, and magicians.
These stories tell the struggle of our chocolate people
in many tongues.
Centuries of pain we have had to endure
by the conquering of archives and our tribes
We celebrate this culture with the Harvest of Festival of Yams,
good journeys, rites of passage, and a story of wars
and horrid middle passage.
No two stories are the same.
Voices of Griots rise, find souls,
bodies listen and sway to hear about the details of our ancestry.
Curious eyes screaming loud and proud,
painted faces and mystical masks,
Chests stuck out about pointed crowns,
patterns of purple regal cloth,
Dancing gold diamonds, juicy oranges, and oil in the deltas.
The milk and honey that belongs to the earth
belongs to us.
Birds, lions, crocodile, monkey, and spider,
Old listening trees, the Baobab
bear witness to our legacy, our treasure,
that will one day be ours again,
Unbroken, pieces joined
We will see them again
The drums heartbeat,
Old country free
Beautiful in serenity
in sweltering African heat.

The Ancient griots come down from the mountains
like ghosts on the trail.
Come speak to me about the good things I done missed.
About the things that's gonna happen maybe.
I feel the hairs on my neck rise.
I slap my neck 'cause I feel a gnat, but it ain't that at all.
It's a whisper of them calling my name
An echo of their voices

Gumbo

Three or two day affair. Go shopping
to the grocery store, market and select ingredients.
Holy Trinity-celery, green bell pepper, onions
Chop 'em, dice 'em, and slice 'em,
separated and organize.
A real New Orleans style gumbo comes with love,
but not really with corn or tomato.
Savory crawdads, shrimp,
Crab legs, scallops, chicken wings or chicken breasts.
Spicy seasonings, Andouille Sausage
Memories of the country and rides down south to the Bayou.

Too few knew.... it's all it in the Rue
to make with secret ingredients for lip smackin' pot liquor.
Garlic and spices among other things.
Stir the big tin pot. Warm stove eye. Boil.
Spicy air with a flair,
much room to spare or to share…
Everyone wants to dip their ladle in the big old tin pot
Serve over white rice.
Don't dig out all the meat.
Gumbo from the Bayou made with care and prayer.

Good Pot Liquor or Rue
Simmers for hours. All gumbos are not the same.
Lip smackin', finger lickin' good.
Smells so good the animals come gather around on the porch
To take a peek with noses wiggling.
Gumbo famous secrets, grandpa would be proud.
Time to eat. Dip ladle into the big tin pot and pour.
Rumblin' tummy. Gumbo soup wafts the air.

Carried from summer-time stories from down south.
Great Migration stories
Gumbo also comes in the New Year
Makes everything right.

Black-Eyed Peas

Black eye beans or black-eyed peas and rice.
Go with the New Year's tradition
Dreams and wishes.
New Year's resolution
Counting beans, Gather round the table.
Before we go out. Family around.
Talkin' about what we are thankful for
Or what we gave.
Like Thanksgiving and other holidays.
Blessings for the new year, especially
Family and friends' new outlook.
New future we bow our heads
Are silent to honor
Take homage
A party, a gathering, a celebration.
How ever many black-eyed peas
You take from the bowl.
Say a blessing for each one.

Jazzin' Time and the Blues

When the band came to town,
They brought the funk and flavor
with them,
Brought the blues, slowed down
'Round town
Put on them dancin' shoes,
Picked up the tempo,
Heralded Jazz rhythm of the ages
Legacy like luminous lasting desire
Endless flames in their eyes.
They got the fever.
Shake, quake, mesmerized.
Sultry, sauve, telling stories
Trumpets, trombones, piano strokes,
base, guitar, drums
They all know the tune
Groovin' afternoon,
Curvy sway, Jazzin' dime
Jumpin' time, movin' rhyme
Notes softly fill the room
Lingering, slows down
Caressing my ears, my soul
Spirit poured over ice
That's Nice
Puff of smoke of cigarette
Billows in the air
Tickles my melodies,
Cool breeze
Strokes warm keys.
Like Duke Ellington and Louis Armstrong blowing horns
Sounds like singing birds Ella Ftizgerald, Dina Washington,
Billie Holiday, and others

Wooed crowds make them proud…
When the band and players came to town
They carried the funk with them
and brought the house down.

Finna

What I'm Fixin' to do,
Getting' ready to go to the store
Catch the matinee at the show
Ready or not I'm Finna go
Got my dancin' shoes and my coat
I'm Finna go out and gloat.
Got plans to do.
Dance and paint the town thru

I Finna laugh and drank and hang
Out All night.
Give my parents an awful fright.
Not mindin' no curfew
Sure I'll be late.
I Finna pick up 2 or 3 dates.
Stir it up. Hellfire and brimstone
Dance at a party, rattle, shake and moan.
Go to the park, Stand on the corner
And smoke and toke
I'll scream and yell
Have a ball.
Play Craps with friends
Up against the wall.
No police to give me no correction…

I Finna be bad to the bone…
Perfection…
Time of my life…'til I turn blue
Don't tell me what I'm not fixin' to do.

One Monkey Don't Stop No Show

I pout because
I don't get what I want.
I don't get first place
In the contest.
Mama explains to me
That we cain't get everything
That we want.
To keep tryin' our best.
'Til the best is good enough.
There are thousands of more times
To get it right. To be the best,
To climb the highest
Pass the test.
Make the call, Take the fall
But you gotta do more than
10,000 hours to practice of
Your craft. Sometimes
It takes more than that.
You must never stop
Go 'Til you can't go no more.
Never give up. One man
Or woman cain't never
Stop you if you have
A dream to hold on tight.

Tryna Make a Dollar Outta 15 Cents

When one doesn't have enough money
You stretch and stretch out.
Save it and caress it.
Make it into something else.
Drain the juice out of it.
Get as much as you can.
Try to get blood out of a turnip
Or rock
And beat a dead horse
If you don't have enough.
Eventually, it will work itself out.
If you use your wits about you
And work hard at it.

You Do Too Much

Doin' the most
Doin' the thing you shouldn't.
You know shouldn't be done.
I ain't the one!
Stick your tongue out.
Talk too much.
In somebody else's bidness.
You shouldn't be here.
Don't do that. Why are you pushin'
Puttin' a round peg in a square hole
It's not goin' the way you
Exactly planned it out.
Be careful of this.
Take heed. Go with caution.
Not goin' into place.
Stomping like a bull in a China closet.
Doin' the utmost.
Out of order. Out of body.
Out of pocket.
Out of position.
Out of place.
Relentless in a bad way.

A Hard Head Makes a Soft Behind

Disobedient and disrespectful child.
Most likely to get a whoopin'.
Knocking over something or playing baseball
Or catch, up in the house.
When Mama says to play outside.
Breaking glass.
Who dunnit? The Not-Me-Ghost.
It was him. It was her.
When a child is belligerent
And hard-headed or stubborn.
If you "spare the rod, you spoil
The child."
Not followin' directions…in the right way
Back in the day….

I'll Give You Somethin' to Cry About

After a whoopin'
There's nothin' to cry about
The job's been done.
It's over and gone.
Some sniffles and whimpers
Nothin' to recover or rehash.
Don't start it back up again.
2nd time for thrash.
I'll give you somethin' to cry about,
Says mama or dad with anger in their eyes.
Stop that snivelin' and go about your business.
Licks wounds retreats
No time for retorts. Child still angry about moments before
But nothin' to do surely not to even
Even the score.
Let bygones be bygones for now.
Retreat, retreat, go back to the cave.

I'll Knock the Taste Outta Your Mouth

Even if it's chocolate.
Being disrespectful and talking back
Gets a slap from Mama
Once it happened across the face.
I don't dare say the time or place.
It was all because I did what I did.
Ranted and yelled…off the grid.
Pouted and stomped.
Heated, Determined. Flabbergasted.
Foolish. Made a scene. Only 15.
Smellin' yo'self.
My mouth stayed open after slap.
Aftershock
Eyes and mouths on lock.
Drool came running down.
Look of horror and hurt on my face.
The pure audacity and lack of grace.
That was the first and last time
I was appalled and mauled.
I'd never repeat such a thing
Not that I've recalled.

3 Strikes and You're Out

No second chances. All you've got.
At the end of your rope. No more gettin' got.
Now you've used up all of your extensions.
Time to pay the piper.
Now you see that it's all done and buried.
Don't try to wiggle your way out of it.
Just pay up or do what you gotta do to...
Resolve it. Amicably or it could be messy.
Lessons learned are a blessed thing.

I Wasn't Born Yesterday

Dad said he wasn't born yesterday.
What does that even mean?
When was he born? Oh!
It's a joke.
It means he ain't no fool.
But I sure would like to see if I can
Get away with what I did yesterday.
I sneaked and had a cookie
And blamed it on big brother or sister.
Somebody did it. The Not-Me-Ghost.
So, it really could be anybody…
Dad weren't born yesterday…
He says.
I ain't smarter than him.
She says that I try to be slick and
Outwit him. Try is the word.
I almost got away with it a few times…
But not.

After Dark

It's always
Never Closed.
Run Around and get into trouble.
Children should be in bed.
Adults get into bottles
And jump into beds…
Lose their heads.
Kids don't belong on corners or streets
Lest they know
Consequences and understand defeats.
Sometimes bullets gone into chocolate houses
With children all nestled into beds.
Dreams of Sugarplum Fairies
Fast asleep after milking and feeding.
Dark places, creeping crawling things lurking inside.
Nightmares and secrets know where to hide.
After dark, ain't no good with bad intention or
With the best of intentions.

Ace Boon Coon

Runnin' buddies
They got your back
Through the streets
They jump fences in the backyards
Knock over garbage cans
Runnin' free and wild at parties.
It's the life of the young and old
Wild'N out.
Out late at night
Staring fear in the face.
Taunting danger.
Temptation.
Laughing at stupid jokes.
Go crazy over a girl or boy
Friends close. Blood ties. Pinkie swears
Blood bonds. That's my dawg,
That's my homie…ace boon coon.
Friend for life.
Cold Chillin'
Ride or die.

The Black Greeks

The numbered line pledges
Their life, their loyalty
Their royalty for a
Cause to help humanity and service to
Mankind and womankind.
A brotherhood or a sisterhood of chocolate houses.
Ancient hieroglyphics and Greek
Symbols. Honoring code,
Accepting responsibility for
Community, organization, guild
Mothering, fathering, mentoring,
Creating, Molding, and crafting.
Destinies. Divine Nine.
Giving opportunity where needed.
Challenging, pushing, growing.
No more paper baggin' it. Evolvin' It.
 Showing colors: crimson, crème, salmon, mint, cobalt blue,
Gold, violet, caramel, black.
Vibrant and sure.
Staying up late to pledge and bond.
Running miles errands to please the gods.
Legendary at HBCUs and other dignitary schools
Responds for community,
Civil and Civic Causes without pause.
Learn from it.
Grow from it.
Anchor, bolster and prepare future generations.
Legacy.

Clap Back

Blast you with words
I'll blow your wig back.
Insult me. Don't I clap back?

I get back. Sticks and stones
Hurt me and words do just
As much harm.
Bite your tongue.
Stingin' mouthful.
Bitter. Sour.
Hold it. Sit on it.
Swallow it.
Squirm. Squelch.
Do what you gotta do?
I bite back. I clap back.
No holdin' back.

Snap back. You'd betta pull
Back. I dominate once
Verbally attacked.
Mind yo' bidness.
It don't concern you.
Retort. Verbal retaliation.
It's fair
Once provoked.
Keep your thoughts
To yo'self. If you clap.
I slap, clap back.

Baby Mama and Baby Daddy

Argument with mama and daddy
Sometimes comes around
No wedding ring to bear
No bride or groom
To seal the deal
Maybe shack up a time or two
Gives money sometimes hugs
Complicated jumps from family to family
Birthdays, vacations, recitals,
Parent teacher conferences
Sorted out
Sometimes not
Often Worked out
Whispers baby chile
Seen. Unseen.
Together moments.
Flickering. Fleeting.
Baby growing.
Baby Gone.
All grown up...
No sing-alongs
Baby now man-child
Or Woman
Where has the time gone?
Grandmother, Grandfather,
Cousins and aunts wait around to see
baby pulled to and fro... in and out of
systems.... or stability.
Home life and friends abounded.
Molded by circumstance, drive, and role models.
Life ready to see chocolate baby in worked out or
unresolved scenes.

At the BBQ, Not the Picnic

Reunion
Dad or cousin or uncle
Beer and BBQ
On the grill
Ribs or steaks
Hot dogs
Hear the sizzle flip over the tongs.
Smell the meat.
Corn on the cob
Fried catfish
Sometimes shrimp
Fried Chicken or baked chicken
Finger lickin' good cook
Fried oysters Po' Boy sandwich with French bread and mustard.
A company of side dishes like:
Black eyed peas, potato salad, candied yams, or sweet potatoes,
macaroni and cheese,
collard greens and mustard greens,
seasoned with ham or turkey.
Hold the Chitlins please. Or Not.

Everybody brings sumthin'
If you cain't cook,
Don't buy your pie or cake
From the store.unless you
Wanna get joked. We can tell
If you didn't use real butter
Make grandma or Auntie's recipe.

Kids jump around with games.
Sack races, tug of war.
Movin'

Groovin'
Rockin'
Jammin'
Laughin'
Jokin'
Old Stories, family stories
Good Times.
Fun.

Barbershop

The neighborhood barbershop is supported
To be a safe place, haven
Where chocolate people go to
Find all the action in town.
Men take their little boys
To get haircuts.
Curly hair, coiled hair
Wavy and straight hair
Dreaded hair
Baby hairs fall away.
A new boy
A new man
Boy comes in
Tradition passed down
Who shot John?
Men talk.
Model man, mentor warrior
Sit back in chair, Lean back
Watch the pinstripes dazzled
Black leather seats
Silver swivel stand
Buzz of the clippers
Evoke nervousness
Then calm the stormy seas
Zoom from front to back
Diagonal with grain and swirl
Hair trickles to the floor.
Summer breeze wind.
Blows hair away in tiny tornado swirls
Baby boy moves to man.
They laugh about the manly
Tall talk

Sometimey
Stern looks
Solemn
Grunt and growl
Down low deep voices treble
Sure and secure
Slap hands and fist bump
about the chocolate traditions.

Cocoa Salons

Hair salon full of gossipin'
folks that do the most.
Never tell secrets or those to be exposed.
Loose lips sink ships and mouths should be closed.
Rumors of war, things just begun.
Gettin' your hair "did"
Straightened, twisted, or braided dark chocolate, caramel,
or red velvet hair.
Got to be tight, no room for error to spare.
Hot hair dryer with roller heads sleepy, talkin'
or flippin' magazines.
Women, teenagers, or little girl
Gettin' ready for special event
Gettin' dolled up and lookin' fine.
Fresh cut, curling iron
- clipped and sprayed (gel)
Now you're done, it's fried and laid.
Lovers and such, grand stories of fights and parties.
We just got started don't ruin the fun.
Selling Cd's women's clothes, bootleg.
Sandwiches, chips. and weave hair.
Tumble weave rolls.
Cocoa salons are where chocolate people
Meet to share the news around town
We talk and whisper about different views
We are carefree about the consequences of the talk.

You Ain't Worth 2 Dead Flies

A life worth something
Ain't worth nothin'
But where one does constantly go wrong
It ain't worth a ball of dust.
We live in this world to create and give back.
Not just take. Contribute to society and not just consume lives,
Or consume lies. Be about something.
Stay stationary or wander free,
but be about something with audacity.
Find a purpose, find a cause.
Be somebody.

Kwanzaa Time

Kente cloth draped over the winter table
Golden candlestick holders of the Kinara
Lighting of the black, red, and green candles
Remembrance of the ancestors
Promise of black culture
Clear tribal principles and traditions
Divine essence of blackness
Smell of pine in winter in the Midwest
For me
Mama and Daddy taught me
Roots of Blackness and Pan Africanism
People united under Black Power
Self-reliance, self-determination
Represents unity, struggle and abundance.
"First Fruits" by the way of Swahili
The African drumbeats are calling
Dancing in celebration and holiday meal of legacy.

Easter

Resurrection Sunday
Bright Lilies
Pastels
Painted Easter Eggs
Easter Egg Hunts
Crosses
Church time
Family lunches and dinners
Chocolate-covered bunnies.
Best outfits saved up for
Me and Big brother

New shiny shoes
Trouser socks and flowered lace ankle socks
Big-brimmed hats
Multi-colored suits and dresses
All come to church
After a long sabbatical.

Holiday Hissie Fit

Every time before the event
Rage ensues
Wait to the last minute
Yelling and rampage
Spit flying, arms flailing
Contorted faces
The throbbing of my head
Holiday traditions continue
Never too much or too little
Would be enough to quench the beast
Of mother
Of Us cleaning and cooking last
Minute hectic before friends and relatives
Coming over
Vacuuming and last-minute cooking
The thirst of the beast who
Hunger for perfection
Anxiety

We emerged scathed
From distant memories of tongue lashing and musings
Of childhood preparations over the years
Have taken various forms
Formed out of love and traditions
Of madness

We put up with the adult temper tantrums
And ordering around from mother.
Entertain her to keep her at bay
Save face
In the end it all comes together
It was well worth the agony and pain
Down to the holiday meal
Which is successful and memorable,
A feast for family and friends.

Juneteenth Mind

On June 19th, da captives were set free.
Cap'n came off his horse and proclaim'
We's a free peoples. Even tho' massa say we still slaves.
Lincoln say we free befo', but I heard it took time.

We runned away and tore our clothes.
Da clothes dat he gave dat scratch'd and itch'd up 'gainst Black skin
Da callouses and blisters and deep scars.
Massa jus' laugh and he grin.
He don' know what he done or what he gonna do.
Because his hands soft like a baby's butt and warm butter.
His hands pale, lily-white, not seared by sun,
But dey have blood on dem. Unclean.

Massa wrung his hands to da sky. Why me?
All dis land and no one to tend da fields.
Some stay behin' at dey own risk.
Dey had no wheres else to go.
But massa jus' treated 'em jus' same as dey did befo'.
He jus' work now in the same row as dem. Caught da same sun as dem.
Prick da same blood as dem.
Pick da same cotton as dem.
Now he see blood risin' up in da fields.
Blood in dey eyes, where bodies kill'd.

In da night he hears cries. It keep him up. He destroy'd.
Souls linger in fog. Ezekiel, Jonah, and Martha and Baby Doll
bear hymns and stories dey carry like fabric on dey backs,
like chi'ren clingin' to a bossom for etern'ty.
Dey never be forgettin' those left behin'.
Dey cling on fo' dear life. So dey never fo'get da love' ones.
But dey gone ahead and start a new life freed.
Journey ahead to the Lan' of Lincoln, union north, where a
    negro can keep

A piece of min' and have his o' her own body.
Can be a whole man, a whole woman. Chi'ren sing of freedom songs
And it come true.

I catch my breath. My heart skips 'cause I'm scared. Scarred.
Not dere yet. Da promised land in hymns talked about.
I keep cornrows braided in my scalp
So we can find our way. I sing it soft to dem on the way of
The undergroun'
By the river. Water knows us and calls us to safety.
By time, we go to a place where we can read and write free.
And think for o'selves.

These here will papers make us free.
Oh! Lawd! I knew dis day would come.
My body now broken, burnt in the fields
and slain by Massa and overseer and defiled.
But you see my eyes when I was first birth' into the earth.
God knows how I wait so long. My soul t'red.
It seem like etern'ty.
Born slave, reborn free. Shown jus' as the sun rises.
Now, I untangle and brush my black woolly hair, re-braid it,
and put on the best I knows how.

The big cap'n man says I'm free and I believes it now.
I waitin' to see
what awaits me and us over yonder on da other side.
I be free. I be me.
I be a free woman jus' like my ancestors in Africa.

Dey help me in the undergroun' and we don' rest
'til we gets to da place…
Keep walkin'. My feets hurt, legs heavy.
I ain't got no REAL papers yet.
But I's still free. 'Cus my heart and soul tells me it is.

Paper Bags

Colorism in my own race
In my face
Disgraced
High yellow butterscotch
Caramel, Chocolate
Shades of grey
Yellow Skin
Brown sugar, mahogany
Chocolate, charcoal
Black as night
Paper bag test
Keeping others out
Locking others in
Mind games
On that light skinned stuff
On a plane searching
An Africa that exists
Without shades of paper bag
Homegrown Zion
Dark skinned deemed access. Or not.
Not admitted, discrimination
Slavery mind, continuum
Culturally unequal
Unbalanced dynamics
Skin tone privileges. Deaf tone.
Societies and organizational history
Welcomed or turned away from parties and functions
Tested images of beauty
Crinkled bent corners
Mama brings the groceries home to us
Like curiosity
We pull the paper bag down

Leafy greens emerge
Tomatoes, sweet potato
Bread from the bakery
We don't know about paper bag test until
We are told. We ask the questions.
So, we try to figure out where we fit it
But it already shows around town
Our eyes are opened.

Tap Shoes

Tap, Tap, Tap
Black shiny tap shoes
Goes clickety clack
Tap, Tap, Tap
On a Wooden floor
Music to my ears
Leather and metal
Combine to make beautiful
Sound

Heel Drop, Hop
Shuffle, jump, slap
Stomp, stomp, clap
Dig, Brush, Ball Change
Then, leaping and thundering
Twirling and barreling
Through the air
Footwork noted
Lovely rhythms
Audience goes wild
Amidst the performers
Amazement
Shuddering, clicking, and tapping
Loudly and softly
Percussion beating like Africa
Calypso-goddesses, gentlemen of the Cotton Club origins
Bow ties, black and white tuxes in renaissance.
In vaudeville
Flowing pants, zoot suits
Jazz, Swing, and hip hop hoofers
Athletic, acrobatic with kicks, splits, jumps, and leaps
Legends of the Tap World:

Bojangles, Nicholas Brothers, "Sandman" Sims,
"Peg Leg" Bates, Gregory Hines, and Lady Le Gon
And Savion Glover
Generations of tap resound.
I feel my feet tap tap happily,
The rhythm of the butterfly
Improv beats
Heal to toe, lively steps.
Whirlybird dance
Happiness found.

Black Vinyl

Throughout the ages
Energy makes
A river of rhythm flow
My 45 LP comforts me
And goes in
With Soul in my heartache
Beats make me forget
My folly and my woe
My foolish youth and my foe.
Black Vinyl. So smooth
Grooves, round and round
Funk, rhythm and blues,
Rap, Gospel, Jazz, Rock, Country
Hip Hop to
Make a grown man cry,
Make a lover kill, heartbreak.
Steal a kiss. First kiss, last kiss.
Black Vinyl will make you do
Things. Remember rage.
Good Ole daze.
Home cookin', dancin'
Red light special, basement
Psychedelic
Shimmerin', smokin'
Youth, sparklin' disco, sexy bodies
Black Vinyl will make you lose control.
Be silent, contemplate.
Or Jive, Jive, Sway.
Slick, smooth, round and round
Crackle crisp needle sound.
Needling groove.
Cover magic images.
Remember black vinyl.

Hip hop scratch.
DJ reverses and circles back around
The sound.
DJ honors black vinyl.

I love the way the grooves feel.
Slip into cover.
My record player is a sacred gift,
An instrument and vessel
For my blessed curse and beloved obsession
For my verses
For my strands and scores
Of notes
And romance
Like a Hummingbird
Electric trance.

Chapter 4
POLITICS AND MONEY

Guns, Games, and Lollipops

The ones that play
Games also have guns.
The reckless with guns
Kill children with lollipops.
Lawmakers accept guns
Games and lollipops,
But these can't all be the same.
Sometimes games and guns
Lead to death.
They all seem harmless.
A lollipop can kill,
But less likely than the others.
I'd rather see a child with a lollipop
Or a game than a gun.
A game gives giggles and grins
And makes the heart race.
A red lollipop gives sugar, honey
And love,
A gun can give way to a blood fest, if
Unattended and careless
May cause dramatics and fanatics
Finality and produce
A frightful dying thing.

Blood and Taxes

Tax Day is a day,
I'll never forget,
The day the rains came
and auntie came
to pay me a visit.
I was sick, pain in my stomach,
forever changed.
I ran home and asked mother what was wrong.
She said, "It's time. You're fine."
I'm a woman now.
I'll have to be responsible.
The rains will come and go.
The taxes will come and go,
Again and again.
She said it's a part of life.
That I'm sure I'll never forget,
the day that Blood and Taxes
came to my door.

Missing Black Girls

Where have they gone?
Detroit, Chicago, Los Angeles, D. C.,
New York, Atlanta, Africa
Black and Brown Girls
Backbone of our community girls
Gone girls, chocolate and caramel girls.
Unappreciated, taken advantage of.

Missing lost girls. Lovely girls. Smart girls.
Lonely girls. Little girls. Old girls. Many girls.
Round Girls. Skinny Girls.
Mother. Daughter. Cousin, Sister. Friend. Beautiful.
Black. Brown. Brave. They're out there.
Overlooked. Covered up spaces.
Buried. Vanished.
Missing, Disappearing, Snatched. Misplaced. Absent.
Come from home. Fight for them. AWOL.

Say their name.
We know them. We are them.
Little black girl…won't you please come home?
Your family is calling for you.
It's past your bedtime…
Come home. We miss you.
Who speaks for you?

How the Cocoa Bean Relates to the Vanilla Bean

Dear Vanilla beans,
We've been friends for so long,
I can't remember when we started.
Grown up together
You think I am YOU
And you are me,
Blended minds in the Catholic private school,
Birthday parties, churches
Sports teams, and businesses.
In your ways you say I am more like "you" than
Like "them". You've said.
In a way you have been correct
Suburbs have privileged me, substantiated me,
Enlightened uplifted, elevated a negro.

My position is difficult and not so streetwise.
Sweet wise. Chocolate and vanilla swirled all together.
I've been corrupted and removed from single-mindedness.
Double mindedness.
I walk in duality among you.
The chocolate child among you.
Living in a chocolate house made of vanilla too.
Ruled by vanilla ways and means.
My childhood however preserved with mostly
Loving memories with ignorance, endurance, and promise.
Stamped with the unknowing of the treacherous journey
By which my ancestors were birthed. Until recently.
Not whence my ancestry came only to know
In the mastery and maturity of my years

I speak to the vanilla and chocolate childhood in me because
I walked the lines of duality like a tightrope artist
Judiciously looking down
Looking backwards. Unaware of Sankofa

111

Sometimes not paying attention to the now.
Looking ahead prematurely and not living in the moment.
Maybe I thought things would get better with age.

Some things got better. Some got worse. But I always remained
In a childlike spirit and wanted to believe we could live in a world
Where vanilla and chocolate were equal
And taste the same sweetness and goodness.
In some places, it is still not truth.
We are still colored crayons in the box.
Not considered beautiful variant complexions, shades, tones, tints.
But seen often as a pigmented stain.
We are reminded of our rights violated.
Cocoa colored. We remain.

Have you not known the pain I bore? We bore, chosen to ignore?
The happiness I endured from discovery of me.
Disappearance of swirls and blurred lines of vanilla and
    chocolate emerge.
Does vanilla bean know the chocolate pain?
Vanilla beans are brown too, but their flowers are white.
Brethren and sister interwoven and connected.
Take heed of a patronizing tone reminiscent of master and
    slave if goes unchecked.
Always questioning, discerning

How? When?
Where will Chocolate be equal to Vanilla everywhere?
Tastes the same everywhere?
Vanilla, I care to share, but you may never know the real black
    skin experience,
Milk chocolate side of me completely. Observe and take notice.

Teacher with a Handgun Spells M-U-R-D-E-R

They thought. He just pulled the trigger.
It just slipped. She just pounced.
It was an accident. Just a killing.
They are just bullets. It's just one or two lives.
I hate them. You hate me. She hates her.
He hates him. She's in love with him.
Grab that Glock. Quick. Duck under that desk.
It was fo' real. No… she didn't.
Yeah…he did.
It wasn't the right time to die.
What do we do with this?
It should've never started.
Why are the parents wailing?
Who is to blame?
What is this murder in schools?
Why are we doing this?
Jump on this assailant or shoot them?
Is there enough time?
How much time is enough?
Right state of mind?
Too quick or too slow?
Training. No training.
Blame game. Don't say goodbye…not now.
I've only got one life.
Thank you for your sacrifice, military educator.
"Look at what they've made you give."
Who are we? What are we? Are we animals?
Or are we civilized? Why is this happening?
Who are you? What gives you the right?
Make up your mind. Because in the end…
All of us could die…
Depending on how we tip the scale.

Your decision. My decision. Our decision.
What you think?How they think?
What meds are they taking?
Is it a good day or a bad day?
How's the weather outside?
Grim Reaper or Snowy Angel Or just live.
Be lucky or stay lucky. Be informed.
Get prepared. Stay prepared.
Pray up. Stay up.
Know this. Our lives depend on every single
Person to be alert…
Be in the know…. How did we get here….?

Death of a Jogger

Ahmaud Arbury
A young man in the bitter south
Jogs on a dusty asphalt road
Heat sweltering
His mind on the pavement ahead
He picks up the pace
A white pickup truck
Two vanilla grizzlies
Follows the lamb.
Then jogger speeds up.
Slows down
The cut of his shirt
Shows his muscles
Breathing paced and panting
Sweat trickles down his brow
The vanilla stop the truck beside chocolate young man
Appearance of fear
Apprehension of evil
White fear
A vanilla man and his father
Generations of anger confounded
Entrenched in prejudice
Made a death sentence for him.
Shot gun...chocolate man struggles, wrestles
For his life
They blast him on that road.
Vanilla man bystander
Filming his chocolate deemed useless
Chocolate life demise
Thinking he's just a body bag of meat
Sack of potatoes
Deemed as just another criminal

Unhuman, subhuman
This young chocolate life taken in a struggle
In a minute's notice
Unjustifiable
Vanilla men leave jogger's body on the side of the road
For Dead after desecration of this
Black man's soul and spoke vanities
Over his carcass as he suffered his last breath
Judge. Jury. Executioner.
All in one breath.
No charges at first for the vanilla man until
We protest...
Georgia fruit ripe for the season
Blood bursting for the taking
Chocolate life sweet and ripe for the plucking
Life drained out like strange fruit
How did we get at this place again?

I Can't Breathe

I can't breathe
Because your kneecap is on my neck
My larynx is throbbing
Robbing me of life
Pulsating from other murders
Unreported
Vice
Before my voice
Is stifled
Vocal chords crushed
Silent
No Voice
Constricted
Snake slithering
I didn't know what was
Coming next
Down the barrel of a gun?
But I don't die that way
I just fade away while people
Watch and a young girl records
Pause
It's silent.
Then they rage for me
They say they riot for me
But other black men and women
Still vanish and perish
Blue and black
Supposed to be defending me
They come for me
Flashing glaring lights
Expecting to beat me
Trained to shoot first, ask

Questions later
They don't know me
I'm a black or brown man
I'm a black or brown woman
They post it on social media
Like I'm cattle or an animal
To be observed
Devalued.
"Take it back!", I scream.
But it's all too late…
When will we be exonerated?
When will we be vindicated?
I can't breathe.

Black Mama Sable

Won't you heal the people and the land from the pandemic?
Black Mama Sable?
From the violence
Panic
Shelter-in-place
Covid-19 Corona
Placated fears
Forced to be with families
Familiarity breeds
Contemptuous beasts
Children, parents
Grandparents
Cousins, aunts and uncles
Take heed
No need to simmer, stew or sauté
Fears
Death is already here.
Endurance
Black Folks are dyin'
All kinds of vanilla
Caramel Folks
They not listenin'
To stay inside
Til death the angel of death passes
Over
7-14 days wail and moan
Lost loved ones
Bodies ripe with disease
Truth and plagues foretold
From the wicked we done
The sin we brought
The innocence we stole

They come for us now
Make time to teach to the
Chi'ren now.
See what your seeds have become of you.
The air is cleared
Ozone layered…no more…eat healthy
Save us Black Mama Sable
No stress, no bullet buffet this time
No hunger, no thirst
Death got a new name,
Comin' with the new game…
God comin' for us
Crunch time
4th quarter
To break us down
The high and the mighty
The low and the downtrodden alike
It sweeps through the land
Like a storm
Billiard Ball and 8 ball
Billiard Ball stops
The dust particles settle
Land on the departed faces and bodies
Like the Dust Bowl of the Great Depression
Glass falling, ceiling crashing down
Bear and Bull no more
The chill and sting
Comes and tames the haughty hearts.
Enables us to see when we were once
Blinded. Shackles off, clean and unclean
We await the fate
Of 100,000 more soldiers
Dying on the battlefield
Waiting repenting until
The Lord come to take us away if we ready.

Black Mama Sable, a chocolate woman
Of the people
Some call her mother, grandmother, auntie or Madea
An oracle, healer of the earth and the mind
With her down home cookin'
Greens and cornbread, grits, macaroni
Southern fried chicken
Sippin' on lemonade or a jar of sweet tea
And her famous New Orleans style gumbo
Black Mama Sable is slightly plump
Reminds me of a Black Ms. Santa Clause
She has a hearty chuckle and a twinkle in her
Brown eyes gleaming, rosey cheeks
The whitest teeth you've ever seen.
A smile that lights up cities
Her face is finely aged with gentle lines.
Long pepper gray locks.
She has a sweet soul
But a hearty boisterous voice when she needs to use it.
She ain't afraid of nobody.
Revered by everyone. She is a pillar
A visionary
A legendary woman of African descent
Her touch is healing
Her gaze is inviting and warm
Like hot chocolate.
She gives wisdom and spreads love
Throughout the community
Spreads love and gives the seeds of hope
To the generations of new and old
Weak and the strong, And to the voiceless
She hears their cries. Black Mama Sable

Black Cop

Black and Blue
Double mindedness
Conflicted
So confused
Cause killing chocolate children
Kneeling on necks and backs
Bloated bodies
Blasting Away
At the fray
Guilt ridden about the systemic injustices
Blaring Lights
Hot and cold Nights
Penetrating Penitentiary
Or hard cold Plate
No place for the innocent ones
Children see what their future
May become
Black Cop what will you do?
Protect and serve, tap a nerve
And due diligence to people of color.
Be fair. Get off your square?
Disobey to save lives.
See or unsee what needs to be done.
Keep the creed or see us bleed.
Moral Dilemma. Black Cop don't you see?

Breonna T.

EMT Girl
26 Years Young
Light years gone before her time
Promising baby girl
Chocolate Sister Girl
Gone Too Soon
Police charge into her house
No investigation
Shoot first.
Wrong house. Wrong skin.
No chance she could win.
Chocolate house
Knock unannounced
Raid unwarranted
Controversy
SWAT Rampage
Battering Ram
Louisville, Kentucky
March 13th
8 times shot
Enter without warning
Head on straight 26
Didn't make it to 27
Forced Entry
Already located the perpetrators.
Chocolate Kentucky girl senselessly taken.
We remember Breonna.
Breonna's Law.

Black Man's Burden

Restrained
Barricaded
Jim Crow South
Chain Gang Railroad
Noose Necks
I Cain't Breathe
Fatherless Child
Pressure Building
Black Angst
Hate, Love, Ignorance
Education all balled up in a thwarted
World
Unleveled, Unparalleled
Voices cracked
Hot Breathe
Militant, Peaceful
Held back
Hunted
Drugs, money, sex
Common, uncommon
Chocolate child
Needs privileged 40 acres
Re-winded history
Acknowledged Ancestry
Black Man's Cry-War Cry
Can I live? Can I breathe?
Too educated, uneducated
Black Man's inherited slavery drama
Ghetto problems
Executive problems
Restless, running engine
Assailed, Assaulted

Constitution: Life, Liberty, and the pursuit
to breathe in black skin.
Declaration of Independence from A Black Man's Burden

Black Flies Matter

Take Down VP Mike P
Presidential Debate
Match 10 to 0
Landed on Airstrip
Determined to make a point
Extreme red
Or Taxi
Ready for takeoff?
Voice Be heard
Stayed for 3-5 minutes
Seems like an eternity
Caught the attention of the whole world
No bigger than "a raisin in the hot sun".
But got global attention
Just for being you. Makes a statement.
I wish you could talk
We could see through your many eyes
Four thousand lenses in front of millions
Memes for weeks, months, years to come
Throughout history
Reflection of a VP Debate 2020
Stand up and Be Counted
You watch as Chocolate lady challenger rules
The debate and eventually becomes VP

"Straighten Up and Fly Right"
A Statement to make.
Black Lives Matter and Black Flies Matter too.
Mr. E. Fly
Mystery fly
Took the attention of the debate. Comedy and parody
Material limitless.

Carry the torch little black fly.
Stand up and be counted.
Maybe someone was remote controlling our fly?
Was it real?
Why yes. We all saw it for our own eyes on tv!

Stimulus Check 2020

1200 increments during a pandemic
We wait for the money
We soar and fly
We save
We buy
We gloat
Or We die
Money in my pocket
That I need.
Some add and stack up
For later seed.
For a rainy day,
Some spend, spend, spend
Splendid.
We out here
Bootie to the breeze
On the corner
Doin' our thang
No one can stop us.
We ain't got nothin' at times.
At times we got the world
On a string in our minds.
Covid 19 is just a phase
2020 not a throwaway year
'Til it hits us
Hard, Harder, Hardest
These Black Lives They Matter
If we be rich or if we be poor
Chocolate or caramel or butterscotch chile
With all the flavors, even vanilla or red velvet chile
Ain't no stimulus check gonna heal
What ails this country of its demons

We need truth and no more undercovers
We dump a quarter into the abyss
And hear silence
There's more comin', When and how often?
Uncle Sam,
Chocolate and blended children have always had to survive!
No way you can fill the whole.
But try to make amends with the healing of treatment and laws
Start there...This is only the beginning. Don't count as 40 acres.
You can attempt...
But it still will never be enough reparations for our lost
    generations....
It's just to help recovery the economy and everyone that
    qualifies gets one.
In this case, green don't really have a color.

Word on the Street Is

Watch out for the little brown girls and
little black boys with toys, the innocent,
the pregnant, the elderly get trampled in
the pulsing heat or rhythmic beat
where cops, pigs, 5.0, 12, police and
only "fools rush in where angels fear to tread".
The dead and the strong-willed cry out
Blood spilled.
Jangling keys
Broken necks, Broke backs.
Taut ropes, Broken threads,
Broken strands and strings,
Dangling things, Broken heads.
Who hears their moans and wailing?
There's a new posse in town
in the wild wild west...on the street.
On the Beat
Take the Heat
Bare white sheet
They uplift or tear down the city or town.
Black ghetto, black belt,
Hardened Black man
With a verdict dealt.
Take over the streets
In an Uproar when
Boom Booom! Bang Bang! Pop Pop!
Bullets flyin', mommas cryin'
Onlookers sighin', police lyin', snoopers pryin',
about the terrifyin' and no denyin'
black bodies dyin',
coroner verifyin'
time of death

or waiting for a final sentence.
NO time for last wishes of the departed,
All is sudden.
Final is fate.
The shadow of darkness falls
And devours.
Body cold on a plate.
Body in a cell.
Gone too soon. No lie.
Word on the Street Is....
All about the goodbye...

Smuggled Chocolates

African Ancestors chained
From sales transactions and wars
From 400 years and earlier
Even after the slave trade has ended
Africans still came to Americas and places
In the New World from European ships
On the Middle Passage
Chocolate bodies sought after
Sweet and bitter chocolates
With hearty legacies
Snatched from their lands
Never to return
Never knowing whence they came from
Tasty chocolate treats for the vanilla man
Chocolate bodies ordered on demand
Taken to the killing fields
Summer sun
Foreign lands

Protestors, Rioters, Looters

Protestors make a statement
By marching, signs held high
Gallivanting, through these streets
For the people, celebration of life and rights
Black Lives Matter
Interrupters
Police Brutality
Called for reform
Whirlpool of madness
Cyclones, peaceful
Urging, gathered, mindfulness.
Young and old, youthful
A mother points and whispers
In a little girl's ear we're making history.
Fists go up

Rioters
Violence, spitting in faces
Anger at the police
Jumping over fences
Fists pumping
Urging, heated energy
Boiling pot bubbles over
Powder keg, blitzkrieg
Batons, Shields, push back
Tasers, no remorse, police violence
Emerges again, perpetuated
Black, brown, butterscotch
Vanilla souls tainted
For the cause
Black and Blue don't know what to do.
Follow orders to engage hostiles
And detail or detain
If necessary, lacking compassion

Looters
Unmasked, masked
Hops in and out of cars
Smash windows
Clothes, shoes, furniture
TV sets go bye bye
Wickedness of the young
Hungry beasts
Hungry for evil
Defeated
Desperate
For Reparations
Restitution
Beware of the dog
Beware of the children
Of this revolution.
Unfettered, vile, untamed malice
Determined vigilantes
Crime syndicate
Opportunists.
Born out of and into darkness

Put Your Ballot

Put your ballot
Where your mouth is
Speak your truth
For the poor and the downtrodden
Oppressed with voter suppression
Sign.
Punch the button.
Vanilla, Chocolate, and caramel, red velvet, butterscotch people
Let them speak
They have no right to vote!
They have a voice
To be free under the laws of construction
The by-laws.
These hands we tie, these bonds
We break, these mouths we seal.
There is no misfortune like a country without a voice.
Without a voice, without honor, or without justice
A lie only corrupts the people
Makes the children weak
Generations become mitigated, tangled vines
And partial to the truth
Not caring about consequence
Or concern for righteousness
It's a word I barely see anyone commit to.
Scarce, I look for more
My truth abandoned,
My justice burrowed deep and barren,
Lack lustered and dull
Blinded by my malice,
My jaded hope. But No Jim Crow gonna hold me back.
Don't hold me down.
I still look for a way out of the labyrinth.

Away, I turn my head.
Just enough before the bleeding comes.
We have had enough of the cries of our ancestors of black bodies.
What did they fight for?
They walked the Petit Bridge for us.
Sat at the back of the bus for us.
Waited at the vanilla food counter in Greensboro
And drank colored only water fountains for us.
Struck down by dogs for us.
Freedom Riders give their lives
Civil rights leaders of all kinds
We remember Montgomery, Birmingham, Selma,
March on Washington a
So we could return to protesting and lay down
Our lives again?
Protesting and riots
Broken down by police
Beaten down by the justice system
The courts
The young blood by the hands of murder
While they turn a blind eye to the cries of the forsaken?
When will it be enough?
I see them now.
My ancestors weeping against a blazing sun.
Their tears are dried by the unforgiving heat of memories.
When will it ever be enough?
Wanting...calling for truth...your vote to count.
Stand out. Stand up. Be that voice.
Vote with veracity.
Vote often.
Just vote.
Use your voice to change humanity for good.
Ain't no literacy test
Aint' no pole cat or no poll tax
Aint' no grandfather clause

Gonna hold me back no more
Ain't no bullying, no lies,
No intimidations,
No ex-offenses gonna hold me back
Thank you, John Lewis, Stacy Abrams, and others,
for your "Good Trouble".

Pandemics and Pandemonium

I wake up
Unable to breathe particles
In my brain
Come together forming ideas
Turn on the television
Riot in the streets
Banging and clanging
Police car explodes
Boom. Crackle. Fire. Explosion.
Heartache, head throbbing
Anger, sickness, poverty among us.
I yell out for help and a hand lifts me up.
My friends, my God, my family help me,
Give me a lending hand
My government has abandoned my people.
Shut us out.
Cold steel door.
I hear the cries at night.
They keep me from sleeping
I see faces.
I weep for them in the night. At the midnight hour.
They kill for them during broad daylight.
The circus stays in town
We watch the show
With all the lights and dramatics
West, North and/or South side of town or downtown
on State Street.

Cages and Boxes

They keep black and brown
Chocolate people in boxes
And contraptions
String us up by our necks
Kneel on our backs and spines
Trample on our lives
Can I breathe? Can I live?
We don't get all the privileges like
Vanilla ice cream, no more affirmative actions?
Chocolate and caramel wails
And moans because of the containers of: cages,
boxes, barrels, cannisters.
Warehouses and jails
We have been put into…
Housed in like animals.
Cheap labor. Enslaved chocolate people.
In the body and in the mind.
Lives taken. Laughed at, jeered at, mocked, cajoled.
Spat on, overlooked, and deceived.
No human nor wild beast belongs caged.
Our spirits run free with the determination of our fate and will
Now we push back.
No bars can keep us in.
We build these chocolate houses for ourselves.
Not to be caged,
But to make a home, as an extension of our identity
and true selves.

Chapter 5

REFLECTION
AND LOVE

Wind Turning Pages

My pages of notes
Turn thinking of my heartbeat
In Summer
Memories of Them
The beloved folk
My childish churlish ways
Come flowing back
With a giggle
I sit on the patio
Remembering all the good
Days and the bad ways
That I ever got over the hump
And through the woods
There's a smile growing on my face
As I endure the memories
Scribbling pictures and feverishly
Writing
My hands can't keep up
With the muses of my mindswell
Red robin appears
Building nest, mending twigs
Bustling bushes nearby
Old Red Stairs needs repairs
Needs mending
The pages turn again; cars roll by
I'm alone
I push and pull
My emotions
Become clear
Mother is here
Planting and potting lavender
Mint, Chives, Thyme, Oregano

Chartreuse and crème windmill spins
Cat sitting in the window grins
The peonies have bloomed and spoken
Hydrangeas are pronounced and full
She plucks them and gathers them
A sweet fragrance fills the air
As she walks by
They are ready for the glass vase
On our pine kitchen table
She walks through the glass side door
And not through the big red door in the front.
She places various flowers in the front and in the back
Of the house to remind us of uncle and aunties
Grandma and grandpa that have passed on.
Father walks by the fence and leans on it
With a smirk and a chuckle.
He waves to me on the patio.
Before he goes on his daily run,
He goes to his car in the garage and revs it up.
Zoom. Zoom.
This is one of the good days.
It's comforting and my soul builds up.
I take a mental snapshot of my life
It seeps down into my soul.
On this day we are blessed
Because tomorrow is not promised
And we know that the days are numbered.

When You Go

I let too many years slip away without
Saying I love you's
Although you know that I did
I do
The transition of your life reminds me that life
Is fragile and fleeting
Not to be taken frivolously
Or carelessly.
Gentle like a shell on the beach
Or a baby bird ready to crack open.
Today you are sorrow
Tomorrow you take flight
 Never to return to the cares of this world.
Only to reflect on your time
Here and now
How you made me laugh
And cry
And how we loved you so
For
Being a good friend,
Relative,
Godsend,
Counselor, light and dark,
Funny, caring, generous,
Hopeful and hopeless romantic,
Stubborn and thankful.
You remain in my memories
The best part of humanity.

Selfish Flower

I keep the words to myself
Because they are safe.
All locked up.
Whether sorrowful, Snowdrops
Or happy.
I like them to be mine. A shrine of moments.
Where no one can reach them or
Catch them or exploit them.
But eventually, the brightest flowers
Like Primrose and Pansies
Grow old, wither
When I forget to visit or water them.
And they die.

When children come out to
Play again, with Irises, Lavender, and Lilacs.
In my memories of snowball
Fights, buzzing swimming pools,
And bike rides.
My words, my flowers,
My bouquet of Daffodils
Are revived
In the laughter of the children,
Jumping rope, playing basketball and baseball
Like lively snapdragons
That remind the old and the bitter to be
Cheerful, Lily of the Valley
Urging them to remember to be young,
Before they were jaded and heartbroken.
Then I speak my words and share them.
There's no shame. My Sweet Pea.
I become a teacher and wise,
giving, selfless, and love,
My flowers, my memories,
My Camellias.

The Best of Us

The best of us were never born.
Never here.
Died here.
Lived there.
Been here.
Triumphed.
Loved with care.
Waged war.
Troubled. Struggled.
Lived and loved carelessly.
Things to share. The best of us made our mark.
The best of us, souls light and dark.

A Man of Debate

As a great conversationalist,
He always argued his point.
Given sufficient evidence,
There was always theory and hypothesis to be questioned.
But he was not uncommon…
Too many people that I had known.
The strange seeds that they had sewn.
People that were philosophers
with no court to practice their theories.
Unlikeness and abhorrence to agreement.
You'd say black, he'd say white.
You'd say up, he'd say down.
There is an opossum outside.
He'd say and he never saw one,
So it couldn't possibly be there.
Always having to prove
About spaces that they move
Into
Even when it was true.
Some people just like to debate,
No matter the findings of the case.
Sometimes you pick your battles and walk away…
I've learned a trick or two that works.
Listen in silence and nod your head….
If it's not your time to go to war.

Like the Great Debaters from Wiley College
Or Thurgood Marshall
He'd stand firm and unwavering.
Sometimes he'd be completely right
Other times not so much,
But he didn't budge on the stance
Until his own mind was changed on the matter.
He'd hold on tight.

Heartbreak

Can you calculate exactly when the heart breaks?
Can you see it in the eyes?
Measurable?
Theory or hypothesis?
How do you treat a heartbreak?
Heal a heartbreak?
Seal a heartbreak?
Steal a heartbreak?
The human heart is a muscle, but very fragile.
Crazy in love, fervently
Or hold on so tight and cling for dear life.
Ethos, Pathos, Thanos, etc.
Heartbreak....
Does it crack in two?
Does it make you blue?
Does it find out who?
Will the heart mend?
Does heartbreak in the end?
Immeasurable. Heartbroken.

The 7 Year Man

I met him ages ago
In a place I never expected
At work
In a place with no resolve.
We spoke off and on
Finally meeting for one night
After twilight in the time of the Jasper Moon
Expecting our bodies to be entwined
A one-sided fantasy
Something other than rain.
Nevermind Neverland.

I headed to his home. Driven.
Coming from a past relationship
Sobbing
Ruined the ambiance.

Night extended as we whispered
About our ambitions
Although bodies never twined
No real kiss goodnight or goodbye
No souls completely exchanged, no bodies pressed
7 Man
7 Layer Cake
Expectations unhinged.

He walked away that winter. Many moons ago.
Journeyed out West, to the land of the Sun, Water, and
    Mountain Fire
Lakes unknown
Many lovers passing in-between our last meet.

The years I spent waiting for him to come back
Over the mountains from the West
Riding his bicycle…remembering him being young
He came back…many moons later
As I was weathered by my own trek
Burdened by my own journey
Both triumphant and lost

We met once more under similar
Familiar conditions
Sorrow had consumed me
And he had loss
As well.
At his home we rekindled an old spark
But alas
It might not have been meant to be
It was so cold in Autumn
After I had lost my father in Summer.

Lines now running parallel,
It was then that my lover's alluring smile
All the promise of his rugged, muscular, mahogany exterior
And
Sweltering body heat was no contest for my sorrow.
His strong locks of hair are braided and thick
Like Samson the Nazrite.
His scent of Saffron and Egyptian musk lingered
In the air.

Also, at that particular time
A 25th celebration of mine
Of being out of school

Again, there was no comfort
That came to greet me at the door,
As I did sleepwalk though that unmeasured time…

He said It was 7 years since we first met
A thing I was sure he'd forgotten
7 Layers of memories ago
Monumental piles
Of unanswered questions and emotions
Had Built up walls that separated opportunity

I'm tired of him wanting the bad girl
Wanting to fight
He pulled up and wanna brawl
And argue
Which brings his lust to a boil.
But I wanna be the good girl
I ain't no brawler or Scrappy Doo.

I say "you don't know me…"
He laughs not to believe the hurt.
He goes away again
Maybe for another 7 years
Maybe for good

I wan' him
He don't wan' me
He wan' me
I don' wan' him
We push and pull
The velvet rope until
Hearts cracked open and jaded.
Maybe his mind is elsewhere now like me.

I think both of us
We just tryna survive this beast called life.
His eyes sparkled like a gleam from an ancient rising sun
Once
Bounced off an unwavering, cascaded river…

But
As the seasons went by
The twinkle in his glare
Hunger for me
Slowly vanished

He forgets why he came to me
In the first place
And goes back out
To sea with the other fishes
All the pieces, all the places
Forgotten

He realizes his practiced, persistent charm
Is no match
For my unchanged condition.
Even if I had thought... for many moments
And countless cycles around the sun...
that I loved him once...

Animal

Cold cruel world
Death and disease, despised
Claws and fangs,
Teeth exposed
Mother protects infant
Holding close
Chirp Chirp goes
baby bird
Longing for mother
Feeds Chick-a-dee
A herd storms through
Stampeded hooves
Stock market traders
Under the table
Bear down, Bull up,
Dirty and clean money
exchanges hands
By bribe, by murder, by nepotism
Routine milking
We poison our bodies with things
unnatural, artificial, superficial,
Cut and stuff, prod and stretch
Chop skin
Selling parts
Animal-mixed breed, pure breed
Have you any soul?
We see, don't see.
Black skin-won't fair. Not fair.
Sell souls. Trade bodies.
Sell dreams.
Beast. Survival. Blood. Truth.
Hunger. Thirst. Flesh exists to satisfy.
Animal.

I am, We Are

We are things that we
Can't even imagine
Better than best
Forever young,
Dangerous
Lucky or unlucky in love
Mysterious
Cut off or connected,
Forceful or meek
Wildly blind or visionary,
Frozen or running free,
Committed to chaos
Born of these days.

Kinfolk of opportunity,
Citizens of the world
Motivated to be
The same or unique
Defiant
Fire in glaring eyes,
Wanting more
Passionate
Climbing
Limitless
Inevitable or invincible
Lost in youth,
Lovelier than ever.
I am
We are the days....
We are the future…
Graduating classes

Courageous

Feelin' Courageous
But who are they?
Those that try to silence
A precious identity among lives
That only experience can tell the story.
Gifted and grafted, graffitied
Tattooed with
Pain, hurt, and condition
What made them
Walk with bare feet?

Bare bones exposed
Gather strength through
The whirlwinds
Disengaged then re-engaged
Fighting for the prize
The trophy of battle scars
No re-do, No regrets
Goin' about their lives
Courageous, wild
Golden wings
Silver Bells Chime for thee
The lone wolf licks its paws and walks about
A snow-covered path.
A long, determined journey
Has ended.

Vision

Seeing things not for what they are.
Knowing what they could be.
Feeling that something better
Will come around the corner
Training, straining, braining,
Your mind, body and soul
For a new phase of greatness
Flow of IT
Soaring through time and space
The vibrant spectrum
in your being
Foresight, before night
Sensing what will come in handy
Should All the land Be holy and calm
When we fade into the sun?
No one can know
If the warmth will hold until morning,
If steadfast or fleeting
If copper or gold
It gives its best like a dream
Wanting to be born
Only when mind takes action
Of the body particle
Vision will be revealed
Become a wondrous spectacle of
A Place.
Complete from its beginning to final phase
Of solidarity. Metamorphosis.
Evermore,
Lovelier than when it was conceived.

The Billboard

Billboard in blaring lights
Moving parts, full of darts.
Brazen advertisements
Glaring eyes, lottery prize.
Above the freeway on the road,
On the Side of the Truck
With a wide load.
Way up high message
Route 53, Not Looking
Speeding cars just let them be.
Paintings and soda pops,
Artists, musicians and tv spots.
Trinkets and jingles
That everyone knows.
Restaurants, cell phones
Sweet delights and Vegas shows.
Bargains, deals and celebrity boxing
Fights. Concerts and workshops and
Holiday nights.
Glitz galore.
Old ones and new ones…
Billboards some with fright, laughter
Or bore.
Billboards are temporary,
Purpose is served.
Advertising its way to both
The calm and the unnerved
Pushing to screaming is mostly observed.

Looking for a Black Man Unicorn

A Thing I never Saw...such a man or such a thing.
Maybe I imagined him as a superhero.
But even superheroes are flawed.
Maybe he is married to someone. Already taken by another
Mystified or mortified or taken aside.
Taken a bride. Taken for a ride.
Maybe he's in jail or never been born
Abandoned on the road, homeless or forlorn
Maybe he's torn between a rock and a hard place
On the street. Maybe we'll meet
In another lifetime…
Looking for the perfect, imperfections…
while I'm not even there…
Hey black man where will you be?
I'll meet you at the cafe...I'll meet you there...anywhere? great.!
Bring my black girl magic, pent up hopes and dreams
Bottled up for generations, carried through the streams
Little girl and grown women aspirations
Desires of nations waiting for you
Longing for you to be free and untethered...roaming free…
Take your piece in this world…
Redone image, made over whole, not seen as man-beast
A majestic thing to behold
Like a treasured King or Prince
Values and loved
Treasuring Queens and princesses
Valuing society
Nobility and magic to honor nations…
Way out there…
I have seen a few Black Man Unicorns
Few and far between…
I haven't been able to hold on to them for very

Long....Like a shooting star…
Here one day and then gone…
I'm looking for a young black man unicorn
That can take to the stables and mare with.
A noble steed. They are out there.
I need to meet this unicorn. Because I am a black unicorn too.
I know what it's like to be rare and wandering with
Magic and nowhere to shelter.
We find comfort in our hope and with our sanity
That all of the black man unicorns will find their
Place in the world. And I will no longer be…
looking for a black man unicorn.

Many A Night with A Man in Shining Armor

Waiting for me at the gates
He'll not be perfect
He'll be wise and kind
But charming and quite honest
Lovely and forthright
Like a real man ought to be.
Falseness does not become him
Not something that falls away
When he comes to ride into town
from the sunrise.
To carry me away
To love all my parts
Both crazy and sane
Enjoys the best parts
Of me and the broken parts
Beautiful wondrous and ugly
Truth Emerges from his being.
Because he is the mirror image of me.
He's not jaded, but cool
Challenged to be good
Lighthearted, yet deep
The best parts of humanity
With all of his perfect imperfections.

Little Girl You Don't Live Here Anymore

Little Girl You Don't Live Here Anymore
You can't play here anymore
You're all grown up
And nowhere to go.
Don't look back at your pile of regrets
It'll only make you sorrowful about the what ifs.
How you had to grow up too fast and see things through
See things you didn't want to see
Do things you didn't want to do.
It's past your bed-time
Girl, but the monsters are still up late
Not only the ones in your closet
But out there.
Drinking, gurgling, slinking into your room.
Find a place in your closet.
Hold on to what you got.
The secrets.
Your baby doll.
And the bright sunrise that comes with the rooster call.
You can count on those beautiful things.
Lil Sis you don't belong here anymore
Time to grow up and stand your ground
Stand up and be heard.
No time for little girls with pigtails, spice, and everything nice.
They ain't ready for you girl.
But here you are.
But you gotta grow up now and fight for yours
And I'll fight for mine.
Find your place. Survive. Eat. Sleep. Grow. Glow.
Protect yourself in the day and in the night.
Find a way. You must.

Manchild Manifesting

Hard calloused soul from being deposed
Bone Exposed
Naked Raw cooked emotion
Grappling with identity
Duality breathing
Shallow, then faint
Harrowing recollections
Then not at all
Lifeless
Body burrowed like a ferret
In an unsettled land without borders
With invisible walls
Systematic devices
Institutions try to hold you back
World gone ablaze
Wonderment of black
40 Acres, 400 years
Fuel to the fire
Manchild manifesting
Cries out for momma, daddy
Ancestors don't cha hear him?
Mama, can you save him?
He reaches out for a salve
A chance
But they keep knockin' him down
Baby boy, don't you know
How you gonna live
Hold your head high
Don't you fret now
Don't you cry
Fight for your life…be a man.
Get your voice! Be all you can.

Manchild Manifesting don't
Let them beat you down
If ever you
On your way goin' to see the King
He gonna give you a new glorious
Crown.

Chocolate Chile Anthem

I come from Kings and Queens
Gotta Wake Up Early
To beat the Crowds
Be the Best and be the Worst.
I can do both.
Sometimes they love me if I make money
Turn around shuffle and tap dance for the man
Use my black Cocoa skin to make a profit
On a trend.
If I build my house, do I own it?
Where's my 40 acres and a mule?
How long will I have to fight for this land?
If the catastrophe hits.
This black skin, this dark earth, my chocolate babies
I have protected my children and my home
From the police often enough
Even though I may call them for help.
The system won't let me decide how it should be
Decide for myself
Where can I go to protect from vanilla
Or Sugar-Coated police rules and blended escape
Routes and loopholes
Sordid sometimes by my own chocolate people
On the streets
I wear this Chocolate Chile Anthem like a shield
Across my breast
A badge I wish to brandish and declare.

What does it cost?
What do I gotta give up… my soul for this life?
My ancestors watching the parade of souls
Of what is to come.

I ask them if I ever be free of the confines of these
Corrupt systems
If we ever be free from the discrimination.

Even in a land where the vote boxes
Claim we got a constitution
That protects us from what?
We believe in vote boxes
That are not moved
Vote boxes that cause motion
And Pillars that shake the foundation
Doors with entrances that open
And slowly let us in,
The tv paints us as monsters
A picture of us before we come out of the womb.
They decide too about us before we are ever born
Before we can speak the words
Hear me, hear us now. I take a bow.
Ain't I no different than ones that come before me?
How is it different? It ain't no different.
It's just the lights and cameras are on now.

ABOUT THE AUTHOR

Okema "Seven" Gunn is an award-winning filmmaker, educator, and writer. She's an innovator, creator, educator, collaborator, and uncommon denominator. Seven is the founder and CEO of 7 Gunn Media.

She has been an educator for several years in New York City and the Chicagoland area. She has a Bachelors degree in Psychology and Masters in Secondary Education in Social Studies. She works as an educator, film critic, pop culture writer, film producer, and film director. Seven's work has been featured in The Chicago Sun Times, The Chicago Defender, The Chicago Reader, Chicago Crusader, Newsy, ABC7, Fox Soul, and much more.

Recently, Okema Gunn wrote, directed, and produced a short film called, "A Sisterhood of Signatures" (2019) with the help of renowned actress/producer Cynda Williams (from Mo' Betta Blues & One False Move). She co-wrote, co-produced, and directed the short film "Black Girl Vs. Ambiguous" (2020) with her mentee, 13-year-old Maya Hooks. In the Summer of 2020, Okema wrote, directed, and produced a short called "Black Mama Sable" (2020). These three films have been to over 30 film festivals combined. Also, her monologue called "Black Teacher's Guide to the Galaxy" was selected to be performed at the Victory Gardens Theater in Chicago in November 2019 as part of "The Black Monologues".

The Chocolate Houses We Build is Okema Gunn's first published book. It is the first in a series of poetry books.

www.ingramcontent.com/pod-product-compliance
Lightning Source LLC
Chambersburg PA
CBHW051521120626
46551CB00012B/1017